DATE DUE			

THE
HANDICRAFTS
OF THE SAILOR

A SAILORS LIFE in a CALM.

"Hollo Jack, what are you doing?"___"Nothing your honor;___"And what are you about Bill?"___"I am helping Jack."

Publish'd Decr 12, 1803, by LAURIE & WHITTLE, 53, Fleet Street, London.

323

THE
HANDICRAFTS
OF THE SAILOR

Steven Banks

ARCO PUBLISHING COMPANY, INC.
New York

For Liza

Published 1974 by Arco Publishing Company, Inc.
219 Park Avenue South, New York, N.Y. 10003

Library of Congress Catalog Card Number 73-91687

ISBN 0-668-03441-6

Printed in Great Britain

CONTENTS

INTRODUCTION

This book is about the handicrafts of the sailors aboard ships, manned by men mostly of European stock, during the last three hundred years. I have allowed myself to stray from these bounds occasionally, but it has remained a good working definition. Excellent books have been written on the things made professionally for the use of seamen, ranging from the construction and decoration of the ships themselves, through the models made to assist in their design, down to the instruments of their navigation. The particular subject of scrimshaw has received the attention it well deserves, but all the carving with his knife, the painting of his sea-chest, the 'tiddly work' on stanchions and canopies with which the sailor occupied his leisure, has been given little attention in writing. This is remarkable because many of these artifacts, and here I mention in particular sailor-made ship models and wool pictures, are interesting both as a record of things past and as folk art. A friend of mine who herself made a collection of sailors' carvings, knots, needlework and paintings, told me that her uncle, a retired sea captain from the days of sail, was surprised to see such objects, having been of the opinion that sailors 'never did a thing on the lower deck but dirty daubs and primitive sorts of carpentry'. This brings me to mention that the days of sail are not so remote as sometimes would seem. When I was at Dartmouth Naval College an instructor in seamanship there was able to recall the 'down funnel, up screw, hands make all plain sail' of the sailing battleship with an auxiliary engine; and in the harbour below the College, employed as a coal hulk, lay the hull of the once proud clipper ship *Garthpool*.

One reason for neglect of my subject is that not a great deal has survived, because perishable material was used, and the finished article may have been well received at the time but was likely to have been soon discarded. The things that have lasted, to be cherished in museums or found for sale in antique dealers' shops, will be in general the better examples of their kind. The less competently made handiwork has perished, together with the social history it could recount to us. And social history is what really matters: a finely made professional ship-model tells us only about the ship, sometimes in boring detail, but one made by a sailor of a ship of his own days can tell us something of his seamanship, even his personality. If the picture or model is named, then the ship can usually be identified from back numbers of Lloyd's Register, and her history established. This adds greatly to the interest, as well as contributing to the authenticity of the relic.

Throughout this book I have tried to reflect the people and events of their time from the things illustrated and described. Illiterate and inarticulate the sailor was until quite recent times, but in spite of that, or even because of it, he often had a sure eye and a firm touch when quietly at work in the watch below. Life at sea was hard and dangerous at all times, and the British Navy of the eighteenth and early nineteenth centuries had a bad reputation for brutality as well. The truth of this cannot be denied, but the relations between officers and men must have had their better side, as illustrated in the frontispiece to this book. I am not suggesting the impertinent rejoinder of this sailor would be tolerated, but the tone of the caricature is pleasantly relaxed, and should be taken as an antidote to the Churchillian 'rum and sodomy, lice and the lash' view of the old Navy.

Social history can be read from photographs and descriptions of things, but when it comes to implements the patina given by years of use can only be appreciated by touch. The seam rubbers in plate 1 have this

1 *Two seam rubbers. The one on the left is probably of elm, and is 3¾in long. The date 1769 is problematical, but the rubber has been used. The other rubber is probably of walnut, and is 5in long. Date about 1860*

'tactile value', which is well recognised in the antique trade, and is reflected in price.

The temptation to stray beyond the last three hundred years has been mentioned, and here I will succumb to it. A boat or ship is easy to draw, as every child knows, and the sailor is particularly apt to portray the vessel which is his home. As a result we have representations of ships, often inexpertly scratched on a handy stone, from all ages and most countries. Ancient Egypt, Saxon England, dynastic China have examples, and I remember so well the outline of a medieval ship, with forecastle, aftercastle and single mast amidships, which suddenly confronted my wandering gaze outlined on a marble column in the gallery of San Sophia in Istanbul. On another church of the Holy Wisdom, at Trabzon by the shores of the Black Sea, formerly Trebizond, the outside of one apse is decorated with a number of ships. Figure 1 shows a selection of them, including a galley of perhaps the sixteenth century.

Most subjects, and that of sailors' handicrafts is no exception, can be arranged in more than one way. I could have dealt in succession with the different techniques of carving, painting, inscribing, embroidery and so on, or I could have written against a time scale, but I have elected to deal with background matters first, and then take vegetable materials, animal materials, cordage and textiles. This has inevitably meant some overlap—for instance walking sticks may be made of wood or bone—but the alternative solutions would have raised greater difficulties.

Attractive as they are, and sometimes amusing, I have excluded curios, defined as things brought back by sailors without having worked on them. Such for example are dried puffer fish, walking sticks made from

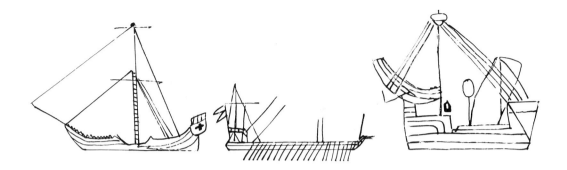

the backbone of a shark, and the notorious coco-de-mer. After a visit to the Seychelles I remember our chaplain regretting, in the sober grey light of Chatham Dockyard, that he had one of these most curious of curios in his cabin. This large nut can very conveniently be converted into a box, cut in half and perhaps edged with copper, and if so treated it would qualify as an article of handiwork and is likely to be the work of a sailor, but cannot be so proved unless its history is known. Another unusual curio is a 'mermaid' constructed from the top half of a monkey and the lower half of some large scaly fish, the halves stuffed and cunningly sewn together. Back in the 'thirties there was a camera obscura and a collection of all sorts of curiosities, including one of these 'mermaids', in the top of one of the pylons of Sydney Harbour Bridge.

Many of the things illustrated and described in this book are fully authenticated as having been made by sailors. Others may confidently be assumed to have been so, from considerations of style, materials, and motifs such as anchors, or naval flags. It has been a matter of judgment to include or exclude some border-line cases. For instance, half a coconut, cut lengthwise and provided with a hinged copper lid, strongly made but without any decoration, might almost have qualified for inclusion, but I rejected it.

Fig 1 Graffiti on the Church of the Holy Wisdom, Trabzon

I have tried to caption the plates with the same adequate items of information, viz: a brief description, a suggested date, one major dimension and the material unless evident or too composite. If a wood has been positively identified I have said so; otherwise my own judgment is given, with a 'probably'. The identification of wood cannot be achieved with certainty by the unaided senses, even if a clean, untreated surface is available, which is seldom the case.

Those people who wish to collect the handicrafts of sailors will not find it easy, for they are somewhat scarce and expensive, but the occasional bargain may be found even yet. Messrs Bonham's include marine antiques of all kinds under the general heading of 'Bygones' in their periodical sales of these things, and there are some dealers who specialise in them. If, however, all that is required is to see and study the subjects in this book, then there are a number of maritime museums in Great Britain, and in the USA. The National Maritime Museum at Greenwich, England, very properly concerns itself mainly with the finer sorts of marine artifacts, but in provincial maritime museums all kinds of relevant and delightful things may be seen.

1

THE SAILOR'S WORLD

Dr Johnson could not understand why a man should willingly go to sea. Indeed the life of a seaman spent crowded with his fellows below decks, only to be called aloft to the masts and yards in a howling gale at any moment, would not have appealed to any literary man in Georgian England. The eighteenth century saw the most severe conditions afloat, particularly in the Royal Navy. Here, for example, is a quotation about food from William Thompson's *Appeal to the Public . . .*

2 Sailor-made model of the brig Patria, *with paddle tug and a lugger in attendance. About 1840. Length of brig overall 2ft*

to prevent the Navy being supplied with pernicious provisions, dated 1761:

That Mariners in the King's Ships have frequently put their 24 hours' allowance of salt provisions into their tobacco-boxes.

That seamen in the King's Ships have made buttons for their Jackets and Trowses with the Cheese they were served with, having preferred it, by reason of its tough and durable quality, to buttons made of common metal; and that Carpenters in the Navy-Service have made Trucks to their Ships' flagstaffs with whole Cheeses, which have stood the weather equally with any timber.

Conditions had been harsh in the seventeenth century, when progress in ship-

3 Contemporary model of a merchant ship of about 1860, known to have been made by a sailor. Length overall 17in

4 Model of the Mark That. *This schooner was built in 1853 and out of Lloyd's Register in 1870. This model probably made in the 1870s. Length overall 25in*

building and navigation created ships which could keep at sea for long periods of time in all weathers. Life remained barely durable until well into the nineteenth century, when improved hygiene, humanitarian stirrings among those in positions of power, and further progress in science and engineering, gradually eased the lot of the seaman. In the unpublished diary of a clerk aboard HMS *Vanguard* 1836–9, scarcely a day passes without some dire event, whether it be a flogging, a man falling from the yard-arm or hanged at the same position, an outbreak of typhus, or a desertion. Yet in spite of

everything the men could be cheerful, and on Christmas Eve 1836 the 'men was all allowed to have their lights till $\frac{1}{2}$ past ten o'clock and there was no small rendezvous'.

I have also read a midshipman's journal from HMS *Cressy* on the China Station in the 1860s, and even allowing for this being an officially kept record, not a personal diary, the difference is striking. The *Cressy*, a steam-powered cruiser, spent a lot of time in harbour, sometimes at General Drill, when bower anchors were taken away in boats and other similar feats of seamanship performed. When at sea she manoeuvred in an orderly fashion with the rest of the China Fleet. The *Vanguard*, on the other hand, when in harbour was for ever swaying up yards, or sending great guns ashore with their crews for firing practice, or landing men for hospital or burial. When at sea she encountered fearful gales, men fell overboard from the rigging, squalls laid the ship on her beam ends. Reading these two accounts, with less than twenty-two years between them, brings some understanding of the comparatively small amount of sailors' handicraft work surviving from the early nineteenth century and before: it must have been all they could do to keep alive.

This book being concerned with leisure, it may well be asked why the sailor of any epoch had time not spent working, eating, or sleeping. The answer lies with two forces beyond the control of his masters—the weather and the enemy. All ships must be manned to cope with foul weather, and warships must be manned to fight with their whole armament. For any kind of ship a 'prime state' may be discerned, requiring the

maximum complement. For a 'wooden wall' battleship it was action stations; for a whaler it was all boats away whaling; for an aircraft carrier it is a programme of full and continuous operational flying. Clearly conditions requiring maximum intensity do not always prevail, so there remains idle time. This can be absorbed to some extent by secondary tasks such as cleaning ship, but even so, aboard a whaler in passage, or a man-of-war in the doldrums, to give two examples, men would have the time to make or decorate things if they had the spirit and the inclination.

With the exception of men aboard nine-

5 Model of a clipper ship of the 1860s, reputed to have been made on board for sale to emigrants. The masts and yards are of bone. Length overall 16½in

6 *Sewing box of wood, probably mahogany, trimmed with whale bone. 12in long. Last half of the nineteenth century*

teenth-century ocean whalers, in which handicrafts were encouraged by authority as discussed in Chapter 5, the majority of sailors off duty would be content to chew their quid of 'baccy' and rest their tired limbs. The minority were not so comatose, and with a greater or lesser degree of skill took up some handicraft. The simplest and easiest thing for a sailor to do would be to decorate the tools of his trade, that is to say the serving mallets, seam rubbers and so on, or he might make a fringe for a boat's canopy, or a fancy seizing for a stanchion. If more ambitious, the sailor might fashion a model of his ship, or a previous one (the last ship is often viewed nostalgically), and if inspired still further there were wool pictures, embroidery, and

the wilder flights of fancy knotting to be explored.

The materials for handicraft work, the available tools, and the stowage of half-made or completed things, all deserve comment. At the simplest, a piece of scrap wood from the carpenter, the knife from his lanyard, and a corner in his kit-bag would suffice for the production and stowage of some small object. At the other extreme, a walrus tusk traded from an Eskimo may be taken together with carefully selected tropical hard-wood, worked on by an outfit of saws, drills, chisels and planes, and even a portable lathe. The finished product might be a fully fitted sewing box, which would require to be kept in a sea-chest, or some other roomy, secure place. Seamen are by nature ingenious, and could be relied upon to find some corner, perhaps in the caboose of a friendly petty officer, or in the manger up forward in an

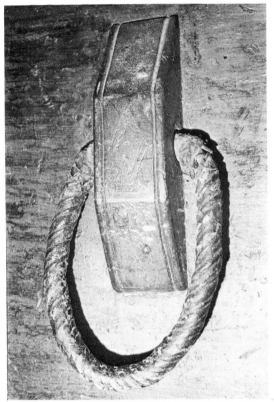

7 *(above left) Sea-chest, probably of deal, in use about 1870. 3ft long*

8 *(above right) Detailed view showing ditty box in plate 7*

9 *(left) Handle of the sea-chest in plate 7*

old battleship, or in a dark cranny on the orlop deck.

Of the multiplicity of things which were made only a proportion remain to interest and sometimes delight us; these chiefly lie between the extremes of simplicity and great skill, and are small enough to provide no storage problem.

Since the late Middle Ages, when the first royal ships were built, with the cognomen '. . . of the Tower', a sailor might alternate between the merchant service and that of the King, sometimes as he wished; sadly often when taken up by the press gang on the outbreak of war, and paid off from His Majesty's ship at the conclusion of peace. The term 'His', or 'Her', Majesty's ship came into use in the late sixteenth century, so cannot be used for dating during the period of the last three hundred years.

It was not until the 1850s that long service engagements, which created a body of Royal Navy men, were introduced, so that it should come as no surprise to find artifacts of the early nineteenth century (plates 10 and 11, for instance) which suggest that the maker spent some time in both merchant and RN service.

The Royal Navy of the eighteenth century remains notorious for hardship and frequent brutality, but there were sadistic officers and 'hell ships' in the merchant navy also, and the Admiralty, paid a handsome bounty to

15

seamen volunteers. Desertions from the East India Company to join the Royal Navy were not unknown. When it came to living space and comfort, however, the merchant service was to be preferred, except for the East India Company's ships, which carried broadside guns like a man-of-war. In a man-of-war each seaman had a place on a bench at his

10 (left) Sperm whale tooth with numerous emblems. 8in high. The Royal Standard cannot be later than 1837, and the Chesapeake *and* Shannon *engagement was in 1813. The sailor's dress suggests a late rather than an early date within this bracket, say 1830*

11 (right) The opposite side of the tooth shown in plate 10

mess table between the guns (see plate 12), and at night he slung his hammock where best he could. It might be on one of the gun decks, or in the dark of the orlop deck above the stink of the bilge. Regulations provided only 14in width between hammocks for each man. Each mess of between 6 and 8 men was the crew of the adjacent gun and, because they must work as a team in action, requests to change to another mess would usually be granted by the Captain so that as far as possible a gun's crew would consist of men who were friends.

Plates 13 and 14 reproduce a contemporary Quarter Bill, and it will be seen that if the ship is engaged on one side only there is double the number of men to serve the gun that side than if the ship has enemies on

both sides. In a three decker such as the *Blenheim*, the lower deck guns would be 32-pounders, that is to say firing a solid iron shot weighing 32 pounds, the middle deck guns 24-pounders, and the upper deck guns 18-pounders. However as the ship aged, the sizes of gun might be reduced. It must have been hot work to serve a 32-pounder gun, the largest size of long gun, with only six men, even not allowing for casualties. Loading, firing and sponging out the gun would employ the gun captain and two, leaving three men to work the breech-tackles and traverse the gun by means of hand-spikes. The use of these steel-shod levers was not popular with

12 Lower Deck of HMS Victory

Captains who valued appearances, as they were apt to score the decks. Against the men's names on the Quarter Bill can be seen their special duties, B for Boarding Party, LF for Fire Party, ST for Sail Trimmer. These would be called from their guns in action as required.

When neither at action stations, eating at the mess table, or in his hammock, and not required to be on deck for duty with the sails or other work, the sailor had the freedom of the gun decks, except those decks where lieutenants had their cabins aft, a part of

QUARTER

Lieut: CAMPBELL

Mn: Rigging	Wheel	Quarter Deck		1st Gun & Op:	
	Larboard	Small	Arms		
Tim Appleby				Axls Kiggin	1 C
Moses Price	Tho Phillips F	Wm Ashton	Jno Tompson	Ben Petre	L.F
Peter Butch		Jas Grey	Jos: Cowley	Neil Galbrath	1 B
Jas Wright	Kn Parkinson A	Jno Kidneys	Jno Hague	Tho: Mills	ST
Neil Galbraith		Tho Wakefold	Tho Darque		P
	Main Top	Jacob Gardner	Kn Brown	Alex: Haustead	2 C
Cunn	Jas Palmer	Jno Hall	Saml Bros	Tho: Molineaux	L.F
	Wm Hall	Jno Walker	Henry Harp	Jas Davidson	2 B
Jas Black	Rob: Bigen	Alex: Davis	Jas Anson		ST
	Ben: Petrie	Geo: Douglas	Jno Thomas	Jas Pagle	P
		Jas Evans			

THO: L: FRED...
C...
Aid de Camps... Mels...

Lieut: Haynes

Leopard Battery

Mr Wilson & to Command ye Boarders.... David Scott Quarter Gunner

1st Gun & Op:		2d Gun & Op:		3d Gun & Op:		4th Gun & Op:		5th Gun & Op:	
Tho: Furze	1 C	Saml Rawling	1 C	Peter Herste	1 C	Abr: Cheek	1 C	Tho: Southgate	1 C
Geo: Rathwell	L.F	Jas Davies	L.P	Jno Newport	L.P	Jno Donaldson	L.F	Jas Swede	L.P
Tho: Paddle	1 B	Jas Turner	1 B	Jas Moore	1 B	Jas Jaq	1 B	Phil: M'Carney	1 B
Tho: Marriner	ST	Jas Middleton	ST	Isaac Jephson	ST	Hen: Ford	ST	Jas Kidney	ST
Jas Hall	P	Tho: batten	P	Jos: Long	P	Saml Marshall	P	Mr Dunnavan	P
Ben:Robertson	2 C	Jas Williams	2 C	Roger M'Clean	2 C	Jas Sullavan	2 C	Rob: Pillum	2 C
Jas Southward	L.F	Jas Pinn	L.P	Jas Tridale	L.F			Mr Holman	L.F
Wm James	2 B	Tho:Lucas	2 B	Wm Manwaring	2 B	Rob: Hudson	2 B	Jas bailey	2 B
Geo: Forsythe	ST	Jas Donaland	ST	Jas Greedy	ST	Wm bennett	ST	Jas Allan	ST
Tho: Gibson	P	Jas Roberts	P	Wm James	P	Felix Mizzie	P	Kn Driston	P
Jas Wolf	Sol	Jas Huzzlewood	Sol	Jas Parra	Sol	Ben: Knowles	Sol	Tho: Goodwin	Sol
Jas Neal	Boy	Wm Bellingham	Boy	Young Appleby	Boy	Ben: Scannall	Boy	Saml Jones	Boy

UPPER
Wolf

Mr Gregor & to Command ye F...

6 Gun & Op:		7 Gun & Op:	
Jas Hamar	1 C	Rob: Davis	1 C
Tho: Burns	L.P	Jas Barrett	L.P
Jas Bully	1 B	Danl Villett	1 B
Jas Cahill	ST	Axls Giley	ST
Jas Lump	P	Tho: Black	P
Jas Burnell	2 C	Tho: Nicholson	2 C
Jas Pruner	L.F	Ben: Owen	L.P
Tho: Wagan	2 B	Jas Riley	2 B
Jas Dwitte	ST	Patrick Curner	ST
Jas Dart	P	Jos: Wright	P
Joseph La hai	Sol	Wm Smith	Sol
Wm Henderson	Boy	Jas Bust	Boy

Lieut: Caley

MIDDL...
Lightning

Thunder Battery

Mr Muire & to Command ye Boarders.... Law: Cardiff Qr Gunner

Mr Wood & to Command ye ...

1st Gun & Op:		2d Gun & Op:		3d Gun & Op:		4th Gun & Op:		5th Gun & Op:		6th Gun & Op:		7th Gun ...	
Alex Marwink	1 C	Jas Howell	1 C	Wm Morris	1 C	Alex: Blair	1 C	Jas Forsyth	1 C	Jas Smith	1 C	Jas Dobson	1 C
Arthur Grey	L.P	Jas Martin	L.P	Rob: Haynes	L.F	Tho: Tubbs	L.F	Jas Arian	L.F	Jas Lancaster	L.P	Jas Brown	L.P
Wm Brous	1 B	Jas Pringle	1 B	Jas Bost	1 B	Pat: Flaherty	1 B	Tho: Grantham	1 B	Mat: Dailey	1 B	Tho: Bunn	1 B
Jas Carter	ST	Jere Launcelot	ST	Hen: Jones	ST	Chas Carthey	ST	Jas Gilliland	ST	Jas Hardy	ST	Jas Cook	ST
Alan Turner	P	Tho: Jenkins	P			Rd Nicholes	P	Tho: Fitzpatrick	P	Jas Leary	P	Peter Malea	P
Wm Andrews	Sol	Jas burns	Sol	Isaac Ballister	Sol	Jas Shepherd	Sol	Jas Tansley	Sol	Jas Bannister	Sol	Tho: Kelly	Sol
Jas Moore 5	2 C	Jas James	2 C	Geo: Leslie	2 C	Jas Brown	2 C	Jas Ward	2 C	Jas Cole	2 C	Edwd Casey	2 C
Wm Grindall	L.F	Cornelis Cronoun	L.F	Wm Thompson	L.F	Sal: Spitore	L.F	Jas Coulby	L.P	Wm Rafael	L.P	Jas Oakley	L.P
Tho: Morgan	2 B	Nic: Scofield	2 B	Tho: Atkinson	2 B	Jas bennett	2 B	Jas Evison	2 B	Geo:Davis	2 B	Chas Jackson	2 B
Carol: Leonard	ST	Wm bell	ST	Chris: Duff	ST	Tho: Martines	ST	Jas Boyce	ST	Jas Hardy	ST	Isaac Leatherles	ST
	P	Jas Tapp	P	Mr Bowling	P	Jas Dowling	P	Tho: Boggett	P	Mat: Molineaux	P	Jas Odell	P
Jas Kent	Sol	Jas Ellinford	Sol	Wm Poole	Sol	Dennis Carleton	Sol	Benj: Timpson	Sol	Jas Krasha	Sol	Jas Diggle	Sol

BILL

M.r EVANS

2.nd Gun & Op:	Poop — Small Arms	Wheel Starboard	& on y.e Poop
Ja.s Quick	Lieu.t Tucker	Ja.s M.c Farlane	Ja.s Saunders
W.m Handy	Ja.s Diggle		Kat: Kokenys
Jas: Courage	Ja.s Graham		Jos: Angel
Jn.o Marriner	Cahill	Jn.o Abbott	Make & Attend Signals
	Cook		M.r Smith
	Cole		
Ben: Smart	Paterson	Mizen Top	M.r Crawford
Tho: Light	Tansley		Isaac Brookbank
W.m Fortitude	Crampton	Rob: Blackers	C.J. Kraces
	Jn.o Kent		Dav: Butler
Ja.s Turner	Ja.s Ellinford,	Dav: Kitte	Jn.o Brown
	Dennis Carleton		
	Jn.o Brasha		

DECK — Lieu.t Hetherill
Panther Battery

Agnus M.c Donald Q.r Gunner   M.c Neil & to Command y.e Sail trimmers .... Geo: Bolton Q.r Gunner

9.th Gun & Op:	10.th Gun & Op:	11.th Gun & Op:	12.th Gun & Op:	13.th Gun & Op:	14.th Gun & Op:	15.th Gun & Op:
1C	Tho: Lester 1C	Alex: Johnson 1C	And.w Larmount 1C	Ja.s Barton 1C	Dav: Griffiths 1C	W.m Spears 1C
Tho: Collins LF	Rob: Morgan LF	W.m Warrand LF	Jos: Midlans LF	Edw.r Turner LF	Rob: Finley LF	W.m Griffin LF
1B	W.m Tonson 1B	Ra.t Walsh 1B	Jn.o Savage 1B	Nich: Harris 1B	Ra.t Kiley 1B	Ja.s Chalanger 1B
ST	Jn.o Bevill ST	Jn.o Wilson ST	Dan: Sullovan ST	Geo: Lovell ST	Tho: Howard ST	Pat: Leeson ST
W.m Black P	Isaac East P	Jn.o Perry P	Bryan Morris P	W.m Tuney P	Tho: Murphy P	Jn.o Long P
Jos: Robertson 2C	Jn.o Scolington 2C	W.m Cole 2C	Ben: Robertson 2C	W.m Lore 2C	Jn.o Moore 2C	Peter Parker 2C
Jn.o Bonice LF	Dav: Stevens LF	Geo: Galoa LF	Ben: Bevan LF	G: Shibcrest LF	Mat: Redman LF	M.c Galea LF
Jn.o Wood 2B	Geo: Letteliar 2B	Martin Murphy 2B	Ja.s Kigan 2B	Mat: Wadderson 2B	Jas: Siddens 2B	Geo: Poole 2B
Rob: Lewis ST	Jn.o Gratina ST	Moses Adams ST	J.s Mercur ST	And: Ferara ST	Gavin Tompson ST	Jn.o Brochall ST
Jas: Aitle P	Tho: Man P	Jn.o West P	Jn.o Neil P	Ab: Martin P	Tho: Crare P	Geo: Skymer P
Jn.o Bryan Sol	W.m Ireland Sol	Simon Butler Sol	Jn.s Lane Sol	W.m Robinson Sol	Bryan M.c Cann Sol	Jn.s Cuthbert Sol
Boy	Boy	W.m Banner Boy	Boy	Boy	Boy	Boy

DECK — Lieu.t Wilkins
Spitfire Battery

Workman Q.r Gunner   M.c Gregory & to Command y.e Sail trimmers .... Geo: Hinton Q.r Gunners

8.th Gun & Op:	9.th Gun & Op:	10.th Gun & Op:	11.th Gun & Op:	12.th Gun & Op:	13.th Gun & Op:	14.th Gun & Op:
1C	James Paine 1C	Ja.s Denham 1C	Hugh West 1C	Sam.l Sainsbure 1C	Roan Carr 1C	Geo: Tompson 1C
LF	Jn.o Brown LF	Jn.o Knight LF	David Knight LF	Celestenia Moseat LF	Jeff: Pickers LF	Jere: Fountain LF
1B	Dav: Tullovan 1B	Tho: Irvine 1B	Hugh Bumbly 1B	Tho: M.c Farlane 1B	W.m Tomlin 1B	Leo: Pestill 1B
ST	Geo: Moseat ST	W.m Williams ST	Isaac Newstaff ST	Mat: Hanlan ST	Chas: M.c Crenche ST	Art: Stacey ST
P	Geo: Graham P	Ja.s Baker P	Ja.s Wade P	Ja.s Arscott P	Jn.o Lawston P	And: Wilson P
Sol	Tho: Oldman Sol	Ra.t Robinson Sol	W.m Tomlinson Sol	Jn.o Ward Sol	Tho: Walton Sol	Mat: Newman Sol
Campbell 2C	Geo: Simpson 2C	Alex: M.c Clean 2C	Tho: Thomson 2C	W.m Hillier 2C	Ja.s Lake 2C	Ben: Powell 2C
LF	And.w Bryan LF	Salve Paquet LF	W.m Scarff LF	Jere: Handle LF	W.m Cain LF	Jn.o Peters LF
2B	Jn.o Nicholas 2B	Jn.o Boyle 2B	W.m Stace 2B	Edw.d Burton 2B	Ra.t Heritage 2B	Pat: Duffy 2B
ST	Ja.s Cook ST	Tho: Parre ST	Cha.s Stanely ST	Ja.s Shephard ST	John William ST	Geo: Harrison ST
P	Jn.o Weymouth P	Jn.o Rouch P	W.m Price P	W.m Tucker P	Jos: Percival P	Jn.o Aston P
	Geo: Grindall Sol	Tho: Pemberton Sol	Rob: Loyce Sol	Tho: Smith Sol	Jn.o Read Sol	Ja.s Scearlet Sol

Mr Neil to Command ye Sail trimmers..... Geo: Bolton Qr Gunner										
11th Gun ye Op:		12 Gun ye Op:		13th Gun ye Op:		14th Gun ye Op:		15th Gun ye Op:	
Alex: Johnson	1C	And: Larmount	1C	Jas Barton	1C	Dav: Griffiths	1C	Jas Spears	1C
Wm Warrand	LP	Jas Mullans	LP	Edw Turner	LP	Rob: Finley	LP	Wm Griffin	LP
Kd Walsh	1B	Jas Savage	1B	Nich: Harris	1B	Ed Kiley	1B	Jas Chalenger	1B
Jas Wilson	ST	Danl Sullavan	ST	Geo: Lovell	ST	Thos Howard	ST	Pat: Leeson	ST
Jas Perry	P	Bryan Morris	P	Wm Toomey	P	Thos Murphy	P	Jas Long	P
Wm Cole	2C	Hen: Robertson	2C	Wm Lee	2C	Jas Moore	2C	Peter Parker	2C
Geo: Galon	LP	Hen: Bevan	LP	G. Shiberels	LP	Mat: Kerlman	LP	Mc Galea	LP
Martin Murphy	2B	Jas Kigan	2B	Mat: Wadderson	2B	Jos: Siddons	2B	Geo: Poole	2B
Moses Adams	ST	Jas Mercur	ST	Ant: Ferara	ST	Gavin Tompson	ST	Jos Brochall	ST
Jas West	P	Jas Neil	P	Ab: Martin	P	Thos Crave	P	Geo: Skynner	P
Simon Butler	Sol	Jas Lane	Sol	Wm Robinson	Sol	Bryan Mc Cann	Sol	Jas Gilbert	Sol
Wm Bonner	Boy		Boy		Boy		Boy		Boy

13 (*previous page*) *Quarter Bill of HMS Blenheim, a 2nd rate, commissioned 1762, fought at the Battle of Cape St Vincent 1797, foundered 1807 in the Indian Ocean. This Bill late eighteenth century*

14 (above) *Detail from Quarter Bill, showing manning of one battery*

which was reserved for them to promenade.

By comparison, merchant service living conditions were almost luxurious, with box bunks in the fo'c'sle or deck cabins, but below decks the cargo would take up the remaining space, and the requirements of trade meant long voyages often in tempestuous seas.

It is an article of faith to landsmen that every sailor had his sea-chest with him on board, but research into the matter has not led me to that conclusion. A sea-chest is of wood with rope handles at each end, the sides and bottom preferably of tongue-and-grooved planks, but certainly tarred or painted to keep out the wet. I am prepared to believe that these were used in the eighteenth century—indeed there is literary evidence to that effect—but those chests I have seen, and the one I myself own, are from the nineteenth century.

To support the proposition that the sea-chests of seamen were carried aboard warships in the days of sail we have a well-known recruiting poster, that of Lieut. James Ayscough of the *Bellona*, date about 1790, in which reads: 'Able Seamen will receive Three Pounds Bounty, and Ordinary Seamen Two Pounds, with Conduct-Money, and their Chests, Bedding etc. sent Carriage free.' There is also a caricature of about 1800 showing a scene aboard a man-of-war, having a sailor reading a letter addressed to 'Jack Junk', clearly himself, and seated on a sea-chest with the same name on it. Unfortunately neither recruiting officers nor caricaturists have been renowned for truth. Lieutenant Ayscough was determined to man the King's ships by fair means or foul, and as for the caricature, in this day and age a convict is still shown wearing a suit lecorated with broad arrows, although to my personal knowledge such style of dress was out of fashion forty years ago.

I have seen no serious contemporary picture of a sailor's sea-chest aboard a ship, and indeed there would plainly be no room for such a thing in his berth between the guns. But I have seen the print of a picture which shows what appears to be kit-bags hanging on the ship's side in this place and I believe that was normally where the Naval seaman kept his spare suit and anything else other than the clothes he stood up in. It is, however, recorded that in some ships, chests were stowed in racks on the orlop deck, and accessible at stated times. Like so many other things in the old Navy, this concession would depend on the will of the Captain. Before the days of radio they were complete autocrats. I have just read of one who, in 1837, stopped all smoking aboard his ship because a midshipman was detected smoking out of permitted hours. That Captain, I may add, had himself been laid off smoking by doctor's orders.

Returning to the subject of sea-chests, the sailor aboard a merchant ship would be permitted a sea-chest in his berth, and it is specimens of these chests, often decorated by the owner, which are described later in this book.

Of course artizans, such as carpenters, had chests for their tools, and officers had chests for their belongings. I have an officer's chest made of cedar-wood, with recessed brass handles and escutcheon. This has been painted, some time last century, probably by an 'ornamental painter' such as was to be found in most large towns, with Elizabethan ships and a portrait of that Queen. There are also to be found the chests of whaling ship officers, inlaid with scenes of whales and so forth. Neither of these classes of chest can be taken as sailors' handicrafts, so I will only mention them and pass on to consider the

Fig 2 The fo'c'sle of a merchant ship

*15 Sperm whale rounding on its attackers.
From an engraving by Duncan after Garnerey*

artistic inspiration of the seafaring man.

We can discern the seaman of the days of sail in the confined world of his ship, often far from home in the immensity of the ocean. The details of his life were of little interest to his contemporaries, and he himself was usually illiterate. Perhaps the picture can be brought into better focus by a study of his handicrafts and the inspiration they reflect.

Just as his life was a narrow one, so were the sources of such art as he practised, and first among these sources was his ship. Professional model makers and painters may give you an exact replica or picture, but the old sailor was concerned intimately with his ship, with what it did, and his part in that doing. So the man-of-war man will depict

his idealised self grasping an ensign in the heat of battle, the whaling man will be seen confronting a huge and dangerous sperm whale. Every sailor with the competence to do so will seek to make models of the ships he has served in.

More than most men, the sailor has two very different views of women. At one extreme he knows, if only subconsciously, Our Lady of the Sea, 'white her shoulders, white as sea-foam', whose smile is the sun on the waves but in her anger she may suddenly call him to another world. At the other extreme he is well acquainted with the sea-port harlots who slake his lust but will steal his watch while he sleeps and, for good measure, leave him with a painful and crippling disease. The wife or sweetheart he left at home inclines in his imagination to be the sentimentally idealised woman, and so she is generally depicted. But I have seen pornographic scrimshaw, crudely done, and possibly not genuine. A tusk may be found cut lengthways, the flat faces decorated and the two halves bound together to hide the drawings. The motto 'Joys of Shore' may be included, eloquent of the whaling man's deprivation.

Lastly, let us consider the sailor's traditional solaces, drink and tobacco. Released from long confinement in his ship, no man carouses more wholeheartedly than a sailor, and in his potations he has little respect for local beverages, taking draughts of wine as he would ale, and tossing down fiery foreign spirits with little thought for the consequences. I have myself seen a man before his Captain, charged with returning on board drunk the night before. The Captain asked him how much he had taken, and the man replied in an aggrieved tone, 'Only three pints, sir'. 'What of?' said the Captain, and the man replied, most innocently, 'Wine, sir'.

The sailor's carouses often get him into some kind of trouble, but scenes of drinking are remembered with affection, and sometimes recorded, as in plate 16.

The offence of returning on board drunk, unless often repeated, was treated leniently, on the grounds that heavy punishment might tempt the man into returning late from leave, missing the ship on sailing, or even deserting. Drinking on board is a serious misdemeanour, except the tot of rum in the prescribed circumstances and manner, which used to be alongside the grog tub immediately after the issue was made.

Sailors have exercised much ingenuity to obtain liquor on board, and some evidence of this can still be found. In the old Navy, ships went out of routine in port, and women were allowed aboard, as were pedlars and tailors. These were the days before 'the sweets of

liberty ashore' were granted to seamen, and, although the rules against drink were not officially relaxed, a certain number of blind eyes were turned, depending largely again on the personality of the Captain. I have seen little oval casks, about 8in long, coopered up of wood staves and brass bound, which might well have been secreted inside the voluminous dress of a lady visitor aboard, and such small casks are shown in a caricature of a boatload of these beauties making across the water to a man-of-war at anchor.

16 Sperm whale tooth inscribed with the figure of a sailor carousing and holding a red ensign. Height 6½in. About 1840

23

17 Inscribed coconut. Major axis 6in. Dated 1793 and of that period

In the tropics, notably the West Indies, fiery spirits were made and the coconut abounds. A coconut shell, if taken young, before the 'meat' has thickly formed, can be drilled through one eye and completely emptied of the milk and meat. Filled with rum and the hole neatly bunged, it could be an innocent enough object to bring on board. The drinking of its contents was known as 'sucking the monkey'. Coconuts perhaps originally used for this purpose may be found (plate 17), some beautifully decorated and polished. Sometimes the hole through the eye has been left, in other specimens the top of the nut has been cut off, and hinged to the body by a string or thong.

Tobacco is nowadays a commonplace article, but the old sailor's love for it was

something more than a simple appetite. We find such inscriptions as 'If you love me, lend me not', which suggests that the weed held a particular place in his regard.

Tobacco was chewed, or smoked in a clay pipe, or taken as snuff. Of these, the first was most popular, and regarded as typical of the sailor. An old caricature shows a Scotsman marked 'I snuffs', a Dutchman marked 'I smokes', and a sailor marked 'I chaws'. The preference for chewing was brought about by the restriction on smoking necessary in a ship made of wood, more particularly with a powder magazine in it. Smoking was in early days only permitted in the galley, a brick-lined compartment where a fire already existed, and even so the hours of smoking were severely restricted. Some relaxation on this rule seems to have crept in, but there remained the paraphernalia of strike-a-light, and fragile clay pipe, to encourage the chewing of tobacco instead. As to snuff-taking, sailor-made snuff boxes are to be found, but it was a thing more for carpenters and pursers and such folk than for simple sailors.

The modern term 'Navy Cut' comes from the preparation by the sailor of the leaf tobacco which since 1798 could be bought from the purser on board, although not more than 2lb per man per month. In the years before World War II the older men in the Royal Navy still made up a 'prick' (a small roll) of tobacco, and I remember seeing them do it. The process involved a few fathoms of spun yarn (a tarred expendable twine) and the use of two hammock hooks a few feet apart. The leaves would have been stripped from their stems, well soaked in a marinade of rum and molasses before being made up into a roll, and wrapped in cloth. The spun yarn was slung from one hook to another, in a loop to within a few inches of the deck

18 Snuff box, probably of fruit wood, $2\frac{1}{2}$in long, decorated in pen-work. About 1850

below. The operator stood astride the loop, wound the spun yarn round the roll of tobacco and bore down with his weight to tighten the turns. The final result was a compressed bar of tobacco within a covering of spun yarn, which could be pared off with a knife to provide a 'quid' of tobacco.

The preparation of tobacco for snuff was professional work, and the sailor bought a thin twist of tobacco, known as 'pig-tail', which he rasped to provide a powder for snuffing.

So much for the scene of the sailor's activities, narrow and limited for sure, but in direct contact with the elemental forces of nature, and the other inhabitants of the deep, both friendly and hostile.

2
IDENTIFICATION
AND DATING OF SHIPS

A name is important to the identity of a living creature, man or other animal, and the more that is known about any inanimate object—when, where, how and by whom it was made—the greater satisfaction is to be gained by seeing, handling, perhaps even owning it.

Some knowledge of developments in the hull, rigging, and painting of ships, and of the flags they flew, together with the changes which have taken place in the clothes of seafaring men, and their styles of hair and beard, will often make it possible to date their handiwork. Plates 10 and 11 show a close dating by these means, being provided in this instance with a liberal number of clues. Information on ships and sailors can be put to good use in the appreciation of marine paintings, besides sailors' artifacts. The dates of well-known painters such as Monamy and Buttersworth are well known, but the dating of unsigned works, or those by lesser-known men, can be interesting, perhaps even profitable. A conventional 'ship's portrait' will show three views of the vessel, seen from the side in the middle, from the bows on the viewer's left, and from the stern on his right. This presentation gives excellent opportunity to observe detail, but unless the convention is understood it can look like the moment before a serious collision between three different ships.

It is clearly desirable to write a consecutive account, but without trying to follow too many threads at the same time, such as men-of-war and merchant ships, British and foreign vessels, it cannot be done simply. Merchant ships only become of importance, from the viewpoint of this book, in the nineteenth century, and the differences between British and foreign ships of war were marginal in the seventeenth and eighteenth centuries. So I have dealt with warships first, then gathered up the theme of merchant ships, and finally commented on the flags used by all British ships.

First then let us consider the ship, and here at once is a point of interest, for the word 'ship' in the days of sail was applied specifically to a vessel with three masts, having square sails on all of them. A barque and barquentine also have three masts, the after mast on the barque being rigged with for-and-aft sails, and the two after masts being so rigged on the barquentine. The brig has two masts, both square rigged, and the brigantine has her after mast with fore-and-aft sails. Other rigs will be described as they appear in the text.

It may well be asked why there should be such variety, and the answer lies in the conflicting advantages of the 'square' and 'fore-and-aft' sail. The square sail is above all the rig for long ocean voyages. Judge your season of the year and your route so as to be on a fair wind for the maximum possible

"THOU GOD SEEST ME"

time, and your great rectangular courses will fill so as to drive the ship splendidly. On the other hand, for coastal traffic, working among and between islands, and most forms of fishing, the fore-and-aft sail is to be preferred. It will take you closer to the wind, and it needs fewer men to work the sails as the vessel tacks and wears. Thus we have the great 'full-rigged' clipper of the tea, wool, and grain trades; the schooners plying between the islands of the South Seas, past reefs and shoals and into lagoons; the lugger making its way into a secluded Sussex bay to land casks of spirits and tobacco, but able to escape from the revenue cutter down wind. For a schooner, see plate 4; a lugger, plate 2. A cutter has a single mast, with all sails fore-and-aft.

19 Painting of the whaler Brunswick, *by John Ward, dated 1823. This ship was built in 1814 and lost in 1842. The ship is shown whaling in the Arctic, the quarry being humpback whales, which were hunted if right whales could not be found*

Models and depictions of all sorts of ships—now I use the word in its general sense—will be found, but the battleship of the late eighteenth–early nineteenth century, and the merchant ship of the nineteenth century, are most common. Everyone knows the general appearance of the 'wooden wall'; the light stripes on the side interrupted by gun-ports, the full suit of square sails above. Likewise the clipper ship of the late nineteenth–early twentieth century; a long

27

20 Model of the barque Fingal, *made by William Prettyjohns, 1866–1952, one of the last survivors of the Dartmouth to Newfoundland trade. Length overall 30in*

flat-sided hull with concave bow, while aft she is tucked well in under the counter, a huge press of sail driving her sometimes as fast as a steam passenger vessel of the time.

This book is no history of naval architecture, but some historical account is relevant to the subject of sailors' handicrafts. Back in the sixteenth century there were schools of navigation and seamanship at Deptford, Hull and Newcastle. At the two northern ports, and at other ports round the coast of Great Britain, ships were designed and built down the years, but it was at Deptford and nearby that the main stream of development flowed. Here on the Thames ships were built for royal use and for merchant employment, so that early men-of-war and merchant ships were much alike in appearance, although there were no vessels of peaceful trade to compare in size with the battleships of the seventeenth and eighteenth centuries. One limitation on size was the requirement that merchant ships of over 500 tons were put to the added expense of carrying a chaplain, although the hazards of the sea would dictate that no single ship should be of very large size in the days of individual 'merchant ventures'. The ships of the East India Company were armed with broadside guns, and only a sight of the ensign, or a view showing the decking over the waist (whereas the battleship's upper gun deck was open) will distinguish them.

The battleship of the late seventeenth century differed only in detail from that of the last 'wooden wall' nearly two hundred years later. It was in those early days that specifications for His Majesty's ships of different 'rates' were drawn up. The exact figures for the number of guns changed a little down the years, but the following general statement will suffice for our purpose:

1st, 2nd and 3rd rate ships were 'ships of the line', that is to say battleships, large enough to take their place in the line of battle. The 1st rate had a hundred guns and over, with three stern walks; the 2nd rate just under a hundred guns and two stern walks; the 3rd rate about eighty guns, and two stern walks. The stern walks indicate those decks upon which there were officers' quarters aft, the walks being for their recreation. As to the number of gun-decks, 1st and 2nd rates had three, and 3rd rate normally two. The 3rd rate two-decker battleship of seventy-four guns was outstandingly popular in the late eighteenth century. Of the thirty battleships, British and French, engaged at the Battle of the Nile in 1798, no less than twenty-two were of this sort.

Smaller than the battleship were the 4th, 5th and 6th rates, employed on convoy duty, scouting, and so on. Up to 1750 these were miniatures of the larger ships, just as a boy

21 Model of the barquentine Lilian, *length overall 15in, and a contemporary model though not known to have been made by a sailor. The* Lilian *was built in 1886 and out of service ten years later*

22 (*opposite above*) *Wool picture of the 1st rate* HMS Duke of Wellington, *launched in 1852. This picture probably worked about 1860. Sight size 39in by 26in*

23 (*below*) *Wool picture of HMS* Arethusa, *a 4th rate of 50 guns launched in 1849, which became a training ship for destitute boys in 1872. The picture is dated 1875 and is probably work of that period though in an earlier style. Sight size 30in by 23in*

24 (*opposite below*) *Wool picture of the 80 gun 2nd rate HMS* Collingwood, *launched in 1841 and broken up in 1866. This picture worked probably in the 1850s. It has been in family possession for forty years. Sight size 21in by 17in. Signed by 'W. G. Horner'*

might be dressed exactly as a man, but in that year the frigate was introduced. This was a new breed of ship, designed for speed, well armed for its size, but too lightly built for hard punishment. Frigates had only one gun-deck, with around thirty guns, the front of the fo'c'sle curved, not squared off as in battleships until after Trafalgar, and they presented a flush-decked appearance from the side as they had no raised poop. These frigates were a great success, and used by all navies. Nelson called them the 'eyes of the fleet' and had them scouting for him continuously. Operating alone as they frequently did, one frigate would tend to encounter one enemy frigate, and a single ship action would follow, the result being

taken to heart by the opponents rather like a single combat between medieval champions.

A ship of less than twenty guns in the British Navy was called a sloop, or a corvette in other navies.

The favoured gun, until the introduction of the shell gun in the 1850s, was the cast-iron, smooth-bore, long 32, 24, or 18-pounder, which could throw a shot of that weight up to 200 yards effectively. The heavier guns

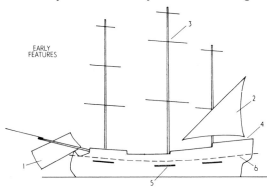

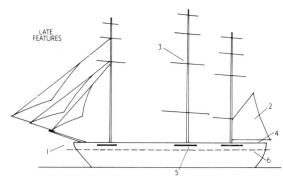

Fig 3

NO	FEATURE	EARLY	LATE
1	*sprit sail*	*present*	*absent*
2	*driver*	*triangular*	*rectangular*
3	*number of sails per mast*	*three*	*four*
4	*poop*	*present*	*absent*
5	*chains*	*low*	*high*
6	*sheer*	*pronounced*	*little or none*

were mounted low in the ship.

In the late eighteenth century there was also the 'carronade', which threw a 42 or 68-pound shot with a much shorter range. These were mounted on the quarterdeck, and could do great damage in close action. Ships could not be equipped with them exclusively, otherwise an enemy with long guns would stand well off and pound the carronade-armed ship without fear of retaliation.

So far we have spoken in general terms about early warships. Now let us consider some of the dating features which can, if sufficient are shown, give an accurate estimate. The dates I quote are British, but other navies followed closely or we followed them. Certain it is that it was only by some esoteric detail that a foreign warship could be identified, in particular if she was heading towards you, when the ensign or the typically square stern of the foreigner could not be seen. Hence the well-known cry from the fore-top: 'She looks like a Frenchman, sir, by the cut of her jib.'

First of all the sheer, which gradually and constantly decreases. Medieval ships are shaped almost like bowls, but the last wooden battleships had very little sheer.

The side view is to be studied also for the 'steps' which will show the break of the fo'c'sle, the quarterdeck and the poop. The poop was abolished around 1815, in belated recognition that the days were now over for a 'forecastle' and an 'aftercastle' manned by soldiers who fought a marine siege warfare, castle against castle. However, to this day the gear belonging to the Quarterdeck Division is marked AX, for 'aftercastle', which is easier to cut on a broom-handle than QD. The waist of the ship was open, between the fo'c'sle and the quarterdeck, up to the end of the eighteenth century, when

the space between these decks narrowed and finally closed by 1815 giving a continuous deck. Even so this feature cannot always be seen as the hammock nettings, if filled with hammocks, give the appearance of a continuous line to the break of the poop. Up to 1750 boats were stowed down in the waist, on the gun-deck, but from then onwards they were brought up and placed on skid beams at quarterdeck/fo'c'sle level, so that the guns could recoil under them and the convenience of all be increased.

25 A British Man-of-War in a gale, by William van der Velde

The typically round bows of the frigate have been mentioned. The battleship gained the same feature in 1811, considerably improving the forward strength of the vessel, and about 1820 the gently curved stern became more rounded. Plate 25 shows the flat bulkhead to the fo'c'sle which remained unaltered until early in the nineteenth century.

33

26 Wool picture of the wood paddle steam frigate HMS Terrible, built in 1845 and deleted from the Navy List in 1877. This picture dated 1864 and is work of that period. Sight size 20in by 13in

This picture also shows several other features clearly, including the bowsprit, which can be seen to end with a jackstaff. Around 1780 the bowsprit was extended by a jib-boom, and somewhat later a flying jib-boom, so that the head-sails could be increased by an outer jib and a flying jib.

A useful change in the sail plan took place towards the end of the eighteenth century, as ships joined the fleet or were rigged anew. The driver, the fore-and-aft sail on the mizzen mast, lost its triangular 'lateen' shape (plate 25 again), with the forward end of its gaff down by the steersman, and became rectangular, with gaff and boom. At about this time 'royals', sails above the

topgallants, were introduced, so that the typical battleship now has four square sails on the mainmast and foremast, three above the driver on the mizzen. Finally, as regards sails, the small sail below the bowsprit, the sprit sail, disappeared in 1810.

Late in the 1750s, on the advice of Admiral Anson, the fore and main chains of ships of the line were moved from upper gun-deck to quarterdeck level. This alteration can be useful if only a side view of the hull is available.

To conclude the tale of the old wooden warship; the first paddle tugs appeared in 1822, and were soon accompanying the fleet to help ships in and out of harbour. The introduction of steam into warships themselves, however, was strongly resisted, because the great paddle-boxes restricted the number of guns in the broadside, and the paddles, with engines high in the ship behind them, were vulnerable. One of the first British steam warships is shown in plate 26. The United States commissioned the first screw-driven warship in 1843 and the motive power could now be taken well below out of the way of the guns. The French had invented a shell-gun in 1824, which numbered the days of the wooden battleship as the invention, cumbersome and dangerous to its crew at first, was refined. When in 1856 the Armstrong gun, with a steel barrel having several iron jackets shrunk on, passed its tests, the wooden battleship was seen by everyone to be obsolete. Soon all navies had iron ships, the so-called 'ironclads', with breech-loading, shell-firing guns in turrets or barbettes.

The fashions in exterior paintwork establish a convenient link between the discussion of warships and of merchantmen. It was in the late seventeenth century that the inner sides of warships along the gun-decks were first painted red, in order that splashes of blood should not show too clearly, and when gun ports are shown open these squares of colour look very handsome. Less delightful is the thought of the wicked splinters which were broken away by the impact of shot on the ship's structure, causing fearful open wounds among the guns' crews. In about 1720 the tar colour of earlier warships gave way to light brown paint or varnish. In the early second half of that century the fashion

27 Silk embroidery, depicting HMS Canopus. This ship was launched in 1897, served in World War I, and was broken up in 1920. The embroidery is early twentieth century. The kerchief is 2ft 10in square

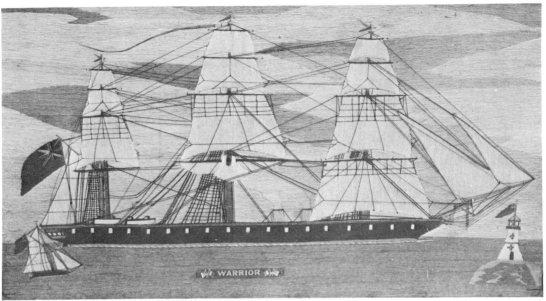

28 Wool picture of the single screw iron ship HMS Warrior, launched in 1860 and the first iron-armoured vessel in the Royal Navy. Date of this picture about 1865. Sight size 30in by 16in

was for painted yellow or black hulls, but by 1790 ships were black with a yellow line along the gun-decks, interrupted by the black exterior of the port-lids. These yellow bands were superseded by white about 1800, and this so-called 'Nelson chequer' lasted as long as the wooden walls themselves.

In the troubled times of the Napoleonic Wars it was desirable for merchant ships to resemble ships of war, and therefore they adopted the Nelson chequer. The East India Company ships had less need for this subterfuge, but even so I have seen a model of one with a real gun-deck and a false one painted below, to double her apparent armament. The Nelson chequer fashion lasted long into the peaceful era of Victoria's reign, going out around the year 1870. A good late example may be seen on the sea-chest lid in plate 7.

It is not entirely true that in the Middle Ages, before the discovery of the lodestone, shipping kept within sight of the coast. There was, for example, a flourishing sea-borne trade between King's Lynn and Bergen. But merchant ships were certainly small, and not equipped for ocean passages.

The Portuguese pioneered the sea route round the Cape of Good Hope to India, and the Dutch were second in this field. The first English organisation to establish trade with the East was the Levant Company, which obtained a firman from the Sultan in 1579 to trade with the merchants of the Golden Horn. Istanbul was at the end of a caravan route from the countries of the East, bringing spices, silk, pearls and similar desirable goods. The merchants of the Levant Company paid high prices for them in Istanbul, still called by them Constantinople, and were anxious to get nearer the sources of the goods, where they would be cheaper. Such an adventurer was Shakespeare's 'her husband's to Aleppo gone, the master o' the Tiger'. But the overland route was hazardous and expensive, so in 1600 the East India Company was formed, and granted a royal monopoly of the India trade, defined very generously as from the Cape of Good Hope to the Straits of Magellan. The Levant trade brought, I believe, at least one word into naval slang, the term 'akkers' for foreign money, which is surely the Turkish 'akça', an old word for a silver coin. I am not certain whether the art of macramé did not come by the same route. The word is originally Arabic, used in old Turkish for a face towel, and I have seen such things in Turkey with fringed ends.

But to return to the merchant adventurers of the East India Company: in 1607 they leased the dockyard at Deptford for a base, and ships were built for them nearby, at Blackwall, where ships for the Royal Navy were also constructed. Hence from the earliest days the great private company and the fighting service had much in common. The custom was for the Company to lay down designs for the ships they would be prepared

to charter from owners who paid for their construction. After four voyages the charter expired, and the ship was by then fit only to be scrapped. The Company had the right to arm its ships in self-defence, which was particularly necessary in the early days of challenging the Portuguese and the Dutch in waters they had regarded as their own preserves. By the end of the seventeenth century, ships of the Company mounted up to seventy guns, and their role became more than defence when in 1739 Letters of Marque were granted for general reprisals against Spain. In 1773 the monopoly of the East India Company was extended to China, and soon the largest merchant ships in the world sailed under the flag of 'John Company' as the Honourable East India Company came to be familiarly known. Time, however, was running out: the power and prestige of the Company was seen as a threat to the influence

29 A Blackwall frigate

30 Dockyard model of the Seringapatam.
Length 27in

and policies of the State itself, and monopoly of the trade to India was allowed to lapse in 1814, though the China trade was still reserved to John Company until 1834, when its remaining monopolies were extinguished. In a way perhaps unexpected the demise of the East India Company gave a fillip to the British mercantile marine, for Messrs Green and Wigram who had recently been building the old 'tea waggons' to the Company's designs, were now free to make and sell or run such ships as they wished. Their freedom produced the 'Blackwall Frigate', a successful design of ocean-going merchant ship, with accommodation for some passengers, which sailed the seas for almost fifty years. The *Seringapatam*, the 'old Seringy' as affectionately called, may be taken as typical of a Blackwall frigate. Plate 29 reproduces a print of her, as does plate 30, a half-hull model which may well be the original shipbuilders' model. The characteristic features of these ships were a general appearance similar to a Naval frigate, the hull having little or no sheer, strongly made quarter galleries on a square stern with cabins inside, the bows bluff rather than fine, and the bowsprit well steeved. They were made entirely of wood until the death of the conservative Richard Green in 1863, when iron came to be used.

The ships built at Blackwall were operated from 1843 by two lines, Green's Blackwall Line, flying the flag of a red cross on a blue square, and Money Wigram and Sons, with a blue cross on a red square. In 1855 ships of the same tradition started to be built on the Wear, but there was of course no conscious effort to keep strictly to the old design, so that the larger, later 'Blackwall frigates' came in some ways to look like clipper ships.

Now we have spoken of a 'clipper', and a definition of this difficult slang word must be attempted, for it has some meaning, unlike the term 'windjammer' which I do not propose to mention again. That was originally a term of contempt for a sailing ship, in particular one that was awkward to handle, and it is best forgotten.

The word 'klepper' is found in north-west European languages, with the meaning of 'running fast'. By association with the clip-clop of a horse's hooves it was applied to that animal, and a horsy man might say 'she's a reg'ler clipper; a chestnut, etc'. Also there are expressions like 'a fast clip', or 'going like clappers', with the similar connotation of speed. So when the port of Baltimore during the War of Independence developed a sailing vessel with sharp lines, raking masts, and a great spread of canvas, these ships became known as Baltimore clippers. Many of them were employed as privateers, and their rakish appearance over the horizon was the signal for many a British merchant ship to make her escape, if she could.

Years were to pass before the word came to have its normal present meaning, that is a swift sailing vessel, ship-rigged, essentially for cargo rather than passengers, wall-sided with constant breadth of beam extended well forward and aft, a concave 'Baltimore bow' and a rounded transom; no stern galleries. The proportion of beam to length was five or six times in a clipper ship, compared to four in a Blackwall frigate.

Ships with these characteristics were first built in the 1840s in the United States, and a few years later by the British. The extinction of the East India Company's monopoly of the China trade stimulated other companies to carry tea and opium, although the earlier ships on that run were not the true clippers

they came to be in the 1850s, when Aberdeen dockyards adopted the American development. A restriction to the building of vessels with fine lines was lifted in 1854, when the British tonnage laws were changed to take all dimensions into account, not only length and breadth as before, which had encouraged a tubby build. Thus a race of splendid ships, some of them a thousand tons or more, with iron deck beams and hardwood hulls, grew up to take part in the great tea races of the 1860s.

Meanwhile the American clippers had been first to take advantage of the Australian gold rush of the 1850s, converting to take passengers out, and soon, as the gold rush declined almost as swiftly as it built up, the clipper ships brought back wood and grain from Australia. The two models shown in

31 Model of a clipper ship, perhaps by the same hand as the model in plate 5. This model length overall 22in, date about 1860

plates 5 and 31 are said to be of clipper ships used on the Australian run in the 1870s, when Liverpool clippers joined those from USA ports in that trade.

The carriage of goods, mail and passengers across the Atlantic was largely in the hands of ships from the United States until the 1840s, when the steamers of the Cunard Line started to challenge their supremacy. Since the early nineteenth century the so-called 'Atlantic ferry' has been by packet-ships, that is to say vessels starting at regular times and, hopefully, arriving with a like regularity. Perhaps because of a certain monotony in their operation, the Atlantic packets have never captured the public imagination, except that the horrors of the early emigrant passages received some adverse publicity, before reforms were introduced about 1850.

In the 1870s iron and steel came to be used generally in sailing ships, for hulls, masts and rigging. Restrictions on size imposed by available timber were removed, and the strength of steel-wire standing rigging permitted longer masts with more sails on them. Now sky-sails, moon-rakers, sky-scrapers, even angel's foot-stools, were set above the royals, and studding-sails and stay-sails abounded.

But these later clippers had a short popularity, although some still sailed carrying grain until just before World War II. Coaling stations had become established world-wide to enable steamers to take on coal for any and every voyage. The Suez and Panama canals were unsuitable for the passage of sailing ships. By the 1880s steamers had largely taken over on the Australian and other main lines of sea communication: the days of the great Liverpool clippers and little Blackwall frigates were finished. The *Cutty Sark*, one of the most famous of British clippers, lies safely in dry dock at Greenwich, and aboard her is the 'Long John Silver' collection of ship models, including many made by sailors.

The urgency of being first home with the new season's tea, or wool-clip, provided the stimulus for the desire to make and the seamanship to operate some exceptional ships. There were others, in other parts of the ocean, bringing hides round Cape Horn as in the immortal 'Two Years before the Mast', or taking emigrants to the American continent, sometimes under conditions of intolerable crowding and hardship. The emigrant run to New Zealand, and Kipling's Auckland 'last, loneliest, loveliest, exquisite, apart', took sometimes six months, long enough for all sorts of personal adventures. Some of the ships thus employed finished their days at the end of the voyage, and I remember seeing a dining table in New Zealand made from the timbers of the ship which brought out the householder's grandfather.

Some unavailing attempts were made to create a sailing ship which would compete economically with steam—for instance a six-masted iron barquentine of 5000 tons could be handled with a small crew, but it proved a slow sailer. World War I saw the end of the merchant sailing ships, except for the 'indian summer' of the early twentieth-century grain races.

Models of Blackwall frigates, clippers, and the ocean-going merchant sailing ships of the nineteenth century are not uncommon, and a few miscellaneous dating points will be helpful. Boats on davits appear early in the nineteenth century, and single top-sails are usual then, so there are normally four sails on each mast. By the middle of that century deck-houses appear on the deck, to house a proportion of the crew: the fo'c'sle remains

40

their quarters also. After about 1860 the outboard chains disappear, and the shrouds of the mast are secured inboard. A merchant ship had her lower yards secured semi-permanently by a chain to an iron hoop round the mast, whereas a battleship had block-and-tackle halyards so that the yards could be lowered at any time. Indeed it was common practice to lower yards and top-masts when a gale blew while ships were at anchor. The merchant ship would hope to have no need for this, being normally alongside or at least in a sheltered berth in harbour for loading or discharging cargo.

It remains to consider the host of small ships which did not normally undertake ocean passages, and first among them in the last century, until displaced by the schooner around 1870, was the brig. This two-masted square-rigged little vessel carried the coastal trade of Great Britain; brought fruit from the Atlantic Islands, Spain and the Mediterranean; traded across the North Sea; supported and supplemented the colonists around the coasts of Australia and New Zealand. Many were built in, and operated from, the smaller ports of many countries. Double top-sails were usual, except in the North Sea colliers, carrying coals from Newcastle to London but proverbially never the other way round. These vessels, also sometimes ship-rigged, were unmistakable with square bow and stern, 'built by the mile and sawn off by the yard' as the saying was. An earlier collier achieved distinction by sailing, as HMS *Endeavour*, with Captain Cook on his voyages of discovery. He had been trained to the sea in colliers, and appreciated their robust hulls, capable of taking hard knocks in unchartered waters. A more typical brig was the *Patria*, shown in plate 2.

The schooner (plate 32) was perfected in the United States early last century, and

32 Half-hull models of a ship and a miniature schooner. About 1860. Length of case 3ft

slowly displaced the brig this side of the Atlantic around the 1870s. It will be remembered that it was specifically the 'schooner *Hesperus*, that sailed the wintry sea' in Longfellow's poem.

Fishing boats of the eighteenth century were small square-rigged vessels known as 'busses', from the Latin word for a box, and indeed they were short and square. The development of trawling out of Brixham brought the cutter rig into fishing fleets, and the requirement to trawl precisely across the sea-bed also drove the lugger out of fishing, about 1870. Then the splendid misquotation 'once aboard the lugger and the girl is mine' remained to be heard only in melodrama.

The cutter rig had prevailed by the last quarter of the nineteenth century both for fishing and for coastal trade together with the schooner. Both types were now built and raced as yachts, and the marine artists of the time delighted in portraying inshore scenes, dangerously crowded with such yachts, trading vessels, and fishing boats.

The ketch rig with a small mizzen mast as well as a main mast was introduced for inshore trade and for fishing, as cutters became larger, and the sail area on a single mast unhandy. It had formerly been popular in navies as a bomb ketch, this rig allowing a good deck space forward for the mortar. Fishing ketches are sometimes to be distinguished by their bowsprit, which can be run inboard to allow a number of these vessels to 'park' closely head and stern alongside a quay.

The flags worn by ships can tell us a lot about them, and help to establish the authenticity of pictures and models. First and foremost is the flag known as the Colours, or Ensign, which is the national flag or a variant of it, flown between sunrise and sunset in a position of honour, such as on a staff over the stern, or at the peak of the driver. A second national flag came to be flown forward in the ship, on a staff over the end of the bowsprit or later in the bows, and known as the Jack. The Jack is nowadays only flown in ships under way, but this was not always so as can be seen from plate 25. It ceased to be flown at sea early in the eighteenth century with the development of headsails, which was in its way when set.

The ancient battle flag of England, as a rallying point ashore or afloat, was the Cross of St George, a vertical red cross on a white ground. At the Union of the Crowns in 1603 the first Union Flag was devised by superimposing the Cross of St George on St Andrew's Cross of white diagonals on a blue field. This was to be flown at the main top in warships, with the Cross of St George or St Andrew, as appropriate to English or Scottish ships, at the foretop. Merchant ships were to fly either the St George's or St Andrew's Cross only. During the Commonwealth the Union Flag was in abeyance, but at the accession of Charles II it was restored to use. In 1801 the Cross of St Patrick, diagonally red on a white ground, was added, in a manner calculated by the College of Arms to do equal honour to Scotland and Ireland. This remains the flag used as a Jack in RN ships; indeed it is commonly called the Union Jack, and the merchant navy adds a white border to it.

The so-called squadronal colours of white, red and blue ensigns were flown by British warships, as and when sailing as a fleet divided into the three squadrons of Van, Centre and Rear, between 1625 and 1864. Warships not with the fleet wore the red ensign. At the Battle of Cape St Vincent in 1797 confusion arose between the Red Ensign and the Spanish Ensign, so the White Ensign was decreed to be flown in battle by all British ships. When squadronal flags were abolished in 1864 the White Ensign became the RN colours, and the Red was officially awarded to the merchant navy. Their tradition of flying a 'red duster', however, can be traced back as far as the early eighteenth century, though the old flag carried St George's Cross, not the Union Flag, in the corner.

The Union Flag has uses other than as a jack: it was the proper flag of the Admiral of the Fleet, and at the yard-arm it signifies that a court martial is sitting aboard the ship so indicated.

When the British Sovereign is afloat in a ship, the Royal Standard is flown at the principal masthead. The Sovereign afloat in his yacht flies also the Union Flag and the Admiralty Flag at the remaining mastheads. This forms an attractive setting, and can be seen used decoratively on depictions of ships by sailors. The present Royal Standard dates back to the accession of Queen Victoria in 1837. The old Royal Standard quartered the three leopards of England and the fleurs-de-lys of France: the lion of Scotland and the Irish harp took their place according to the unions as they progressed. The eighteenth-century standard can be distinguished by fleur-de-lys in the second quarter, which disappeared in 1801. In 1688 a small shield makes its appearance in the middle of the Royal Arms, surmounted by an Electoral Bonnet from 1714 until 1816, and a Crown between that year and 1837, when this 'escutcheon of pretence' is seen no more.

By very ancient custom a warship in commission wears a 'Captain's pendant' at the main masthead. This is long and narrow, a St George's cross tailing away in the squadronal colours, so that since 1864 the Royal Navy pendant has had a white tail.

The story I was told is that it represents the pennon on the spear of the knight who commanded a ship in the Middle Ages. Once again, plate 25 shows this feature clearly.

The East India Company had its own ensign, of horizontal red and white stripes with a St George's Cross in the upper left corner, but the many companies which grew up and flourished last century were content with a house flag, to be flown at the main masthead. Exceptionally, the Brocklebank Line flew their house flag at the foremast. The ship of the Commodore of a line flew the house flag modified to burgee shape.

The first code flags were numeral, and words were expressed, or standard sentences conveyed, by reference to a code book. A Naval Code stemmed from *Lord Howe's Signal Books* of 1782 and 1790, and Sir Home Popham's *Marine Vocabulary*, from which Nelson's 'England expects every man to do his duty' was composed. Alphabetical flags were introduced into the Naval Code by revisions in 1827 and 1889, and this code of flags was in use until World War II.

In 1817, at the conclusion of the Napoleonic Wars, with years of peaceful trading seen ahead, it was thought proper to devise a code of flags for the merchant service, and this was done in 1817 by no less a man than Captain Frederick Marryat, known to generations of boys for his books about the sea, such as *Mr Midshipman Easy*. Marryat's code was numeral, with some distinguishing pendants.

In 1857 a Commercial Code for international Code', as it came to be called, was twelve of Marryat's flags, and this 'International Code,' as it came to be called, was in use with some revisions until supersession by NATO code flags in 1952.

The importance here of Marryat's code is that it was used, sometimes as late as the

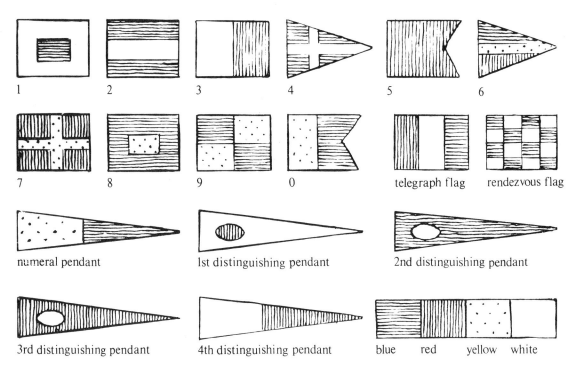

1   2   3   4   5   6

7   8   9   0   telegraph flag   rendezvous flag

numeral pendant   1st distinguishing pendant   2nd distinguishing pendant

3rd distinguishing pendant   4th distinguishing pendant   blue   red   yellow   white

Fig 4 Flags of Marryat's Code

1880s, to 'make the number' of a ship entering port, or for meeting another ship at sea. Every ship had a number in Lloyd's Register, and the appropriate flags were hoisted below the first distinguishing pendant. If a hoist of flags thus reading a number is shown in a picture or on a model, it can be of considerable interest to check the name of the ship. The National Maritime Museum have a full set of Lloyd's Registers, and no doubt they are available in other specialist museums and libraries.

3
IDENTIFICATION
AND DATING OF SAILORS

A man may alter his appearance in several ways, but most easily by changing his clothes, or the cut of the hair of his head or beard. Thus fashion in these things will help to date the figure of a sailor. Fashion is also helpful when we see his wife or sweetheart. For example, nineteenth-century magazines such as *Godey's Lady's Book* in America, and *The Englishwoman's Domestic Magazine* in Britain, had a wide circulation and plates from them were copied on scrimshaw.

The seaman's dress of the late seventeenth and early eighteenth centuries, the beginning of the period under our review, consisted of baggy breeches, for ease of movement about the ship and aloft, with a shirt and a jerkin in fair weather.

In foul weather he would don a 'petticoat', a short canvas coat tarred to keep out the wet, and perhaps an apron of similar material. Behold in him the original 'Jack Tar'.

The introduction of stocks of clothing to be held by the purser on board, and sold to the ship's company, has been credited to Samuel Pepys, but in fact ready-made clothes—breeches, shirts, waistcoats, canvas suits, etc—were made available as early as 1628. The purser opened his pack once a month on the quarterdeck, and the cost of purchases was deducted from the man's pay. This he received only at the end of the ship's commission, and the system must have

caused many a malediction against the purser when the day of reckoning came.

One particular item from the 'provant clothes' of the seventeenth century, the wide breeches called 'slops', gave their name to all clothing supplied by the government aboard HM ships, and the term is still used although the breeches have long departed.

Fig 5 A Seaman of the late seventeenth century

45

GODEY'S
LADY'S BOOK.

PHILADELPHIA, JANUARY, 1850.

THE INTRODUCTION OF CHRISTIANITY INTO GREAT BRITAIN

BY REV. H. HASTINGS WELD.

(See Plate.)

FAR in the hoar and dreamy past
　The gloomy Druid weaves his spells;
O'er mountains wild and dreary waste
　Supreme his stern dominion dwells.

Differing tribes beneath his power
　Unite to own his fearful thrall;
Subject and chief before him cower—
　Priest, monarch, master over all.

The human heart, within his fane,
　Weeps its last blood in orgies dire;
Youth, beauty, pity, all in vain,
　Would quench the sacrificial fire.

Day broke. This pagan land beheld
　A marvelous and holy light:
The glory of the Cross dispelled
　The darkness of Druidic night.

The olive-branch displaced the sword;
　Idolaters their symbols crushed;
The mighty name of Christ, the Lord,
　The revels of the heathen hushed.

His consecrated lavers, o'er
　The old and young their blessings shed;
The heathen spell is heard no more
　Where the Thrice Holy Name is said.

Where frowned the wild, fair gardens smile;
　Where smoked the grove, the spire ascends;
Yet here and there a heathen pile
　In slow decay to ruin tends.

So, though in Christ we are made free,
　A taint of bondage still defiles:
The chain-marks on ourselves we see,
　Like Druid ruins in Britain's isles.

THE FLIGHT OF TIME.

(See Plate.)

TIME, the only traveler that never needs rest, renews his youth by bringing the NEW YEAR on his shoulder—thus teaching the human race the blessings of *endeavor* and *usefulness*.

THE NEW YEAR holds his torch aloft, emblematic of the light *knowledge* and *religion* should shed over the world. Each mind should thus endeavor to hold a torch of usefulness aloft while this year is passing away.

CERES, with the riches LABOR wins from the earth, follows Time, to intimate that *Prosperity* follows *Industry* and the arts of *Peace*.

The *Old Year* is stealing away, yet looks back to bless the Land where only true Liberty and a general diffusion of comfort and happiness is found; and, like a good man departing this life, at peace with all, thus Old Time would wish the whole world a HAPPY NEW YEAR.

HISTORY has concluded the *record* of 1849, and now holds up her favorite work for the LADIES OF AMERICA; assuring them, by the emblem of the *new moon*, that, during every month of this *New Year*, 1850, will go forth, to charm and enlighten its readers, a new number of this Queen of Periodicals, the LADY'S BOOK!

3

THIS dress is made with
of the dress. The materia
body, the bows and sash a

46

STREET DRESS.

a very full box-plaited flounce sewed at the bottom
very rich black silk; the flounce, trimming of the
tique.

7*   197

It was in fact early in the eighteenth century
that trousers started to replace breeches, but
it was fifty years before trousers became the
only accepted wear.

In the 1740s slops included striped suits as
well as plain blue; broadcloth coats; and
breeches were still listed. By 1760 the blue
jacket makes its first appearance providing
another nick-name for the sailor, and slop-
issue breeches are white instead of red.
During the Napoleonic Wars the Marine
Society sent boys and men to serve in the
Navy already provided with an outfit of
seaman's clothing, in contrast to the unhappy
Quota Men, who were rounded up by the
magistrates and haled aboard just as they
stood. Many were wretched creatures, and
their long coats caused them to be called
'long toggies' by the true seaman in his
short handy clothes.

In the early nineteenth century we find
the purser stocks blue jackets with metal
buttons, waistcoats, trousers, frocks and
black silk kerchiefs. The kerchief was worn
around the neck except in action, when it
was tied around the forehead and over the
ears, to deaden the sound of the guns and
keep sweat out of the eyes. In plate 27 is a
black 'silk', as it was called, used as the field
for embroidery.

As to the 'frock', this word has now become
an item of female attire only, and a bit
obsolete at that, but it can be a loose outer
garment worn by either sex, and the frock-
coat, an outer garment not loose but cut to
the figure, is typical of that very male person
the Victorian paterfamilias. The seamen
shown in plate 35 are wearing frocks, and

47

35 Sailors of about 1865, from a daguerreotype

this garment was worn in the Royal Navy until 1900.

Trousers of late Georgian days are often striped, reaching to the ankle, and fairly tight to the leg. Shirts can be plain, checked or striped. Towards 1830 trousers became longer and wider, to culminate in the 'bell-bottoms' which arrived about ten years later.

Even so, the days of a true uniform had not yet arrived. In 1840 the Captain of the *Blazer* dressed his men in blue and white striped guernseys, thereby coining the word 'blazer' for a coat of a significantly coloured pattern.

At this time the short upright collar of the shirt was becoming wide and flat, to reach the familiar square cut of the seaman's collar worn by almost all nations today.

When the Admiralty brought out a uniform for seamen in 1857 they standardised to the

fashions of the time, and some of the first uniform clothing has survived almost unaltered in appearance to this day. However the original double breasted blue cloth jacket and black canvas hat were abolished in 1891, the former to be replaced by a short overcoat. The uniform frocks of 1857, of blue serge and white drill, were replaced in 1900 by the jumpers of those materials which had been introduced in 1880 together with the square-fronted flannel shirt. The difference, often to be seen in old photographs, is that the frock was loose, except at the cuffs, but the jumper fitted the body. Although, as may be seen in plate 47, the sailor formerly had pockets in his jacket, somehow this requirement became lost in the course of the introduction of uniform. From the demise of the blue jacket, until quite recently, the British Naval sailor had to stow small things about his person either in the front of his jumper or in his cap. On pay day he had to remember to empty his cap, as the custom was for him to remove it, and hold it out for the paymaster to place his money on top.

A special word needs to be said about the sailor's headgear. During the eighteenth century the rough fur cap of older days gave way to a tarred leather or canvas hat with a brim, commonly pinned up at the front until 1770, and the so-called 'sennit' hat for fine weather. The origin of the sennit hat I believe to be in the West Indies. It is recorded that the local people there used to bring off a kind of grass which the sailors made into hats. Leaves of the palm-like order Cyclanthaceae, or sedges of the order Cyperacae, which are found in the West Indies, would be suitable. The word 'sennit', or 'sinnet' or 'sennet', spell it as you will, is a puzzle to the lexicographer. The Oxford English Dictionary supposes that it may be a corruption of 'seven knots', on the analogy with 'sennight' for 'seven nights', but sennit is plaiting, and a seven strand plait is unusual. There is however a West Indian fish called a 'sennit', so the form of this word was not impossible in the Carib language: the language now being lost, my theory can neither be proved nor disproved.

Whatever its origins, 'sennit' came to mean plaiting, whether a hat, or a gasket for the piston of an early marine engine, or a fancy lanyard for the bo'sun's call. The sennit hat preserved a fairly constant medium high crown until late in the nineteenth century, when it became lower, and the brim broader. At this late stage it became an indispensable part of the 'sailor suit', worn by children after a fashion set by Royalty. The tarpaulin hat tended to follow civilian fashion, with a tall crown early last century. Both types of hat came to be adorned with ribbon bearing the name of the owner's ship, and other insignia; both were taken in as uniform in 1857 and official cap-ribbons were provided. A flat working cap was introduced in 1857, like the officer's cap of that time, but without a peak, and this developed to supersede the tarpaulin hat, taken away in 1890, and the sennit hat which lasted as late as Admiralty Fleet Order 664 of 1921. See Figure 13.

It must be understood that before 1857 the seaman would wear 'slop issue' clothes at work aboard ship, having access to none other for weeks or even months on end. When in port tailors and pedlars came aboard, and Jack had the chance to buy trousers, shirts and jackets of a less mundane cut than slops, together with fancy kerchiefs and other accessories so that he could cut a dash ashore when his longed-for liberty was granted. From the first issue of slops, therefore, until 1857, some variety can be observed in the dress of RN seamen, and in those of the East India Company, who were also issued with slops. The underlying themes as sketched above, however, are generally valid.

It is worthy of comment here that uniform for Naval officers was introduced in 1748, in colours of dark blue and white with gold buttons. The dark blue and gold remains clearly evident, but the white survives only in the patch on the coat lapel of a midshipman.

Now to consider the face of the sailor. Fashions in hair and beard tend to be the same at sea and on land, with a slight leaning in ships towards neglect of the razor, hot water and time being both at a premium when the call to 'lash up and stow hammocks'

Fig 6 Sailors of the nineteenth century

1820   1835   1850   1870

49

was heard. The eighteenth century was a period for a clean-shaven face, after the full beard of the seventeenth century. In the course of the nineteenth century whiskers progressed down the side of the face, met under the chin to form a 'ruff', joined the moustache, and flowered into the full beard of late Victorian days.

In 1869 an Admiralty Letter introduced uniformity into the Navy, decreeing that officers and men should be clean-shaven or discontinue the use of the razor entirely, and this ruling is still in force. Royal Marines were, and are, permitted a moustache. The typical full-bearded sailor of around 1900 gazes resolutely from the front cover of a packet of Players' cigarettes, with the cap-ribbon of HMS *Hero*. Some years ago members of the crew of the ship then bearing that name suggested to the cigarette company that they might receive some special consideration, but all they got were good wishes. With the Captain's permission any member of his crew may 'grow a set', as the expression is, but if the resultant growth proves patchy, or parti-coloured, or otherwise offensive to the eye, the Captain will certainly give him the order to 'shave off'.

As to the hair of the head, from 1760 to about 1815 the typical sailor wore it long, tied in a queue or 'pig-tail'. This style became identified with sailors, so that as late as 1830 a print by Engelmann called 'Put the Grog About' shows this out-of-date fashion. After the pig-tail, hair of indeterminate length, but tending to be short, prevailed until the 'short back and sides' of the early twentieth century.

4
WOOD AND NUTS

The hulls of European ships were commonly made of oak, notable for its strength, durability, ease of working and good looks. The East India Company ships built abroad were constructed of teak and similar tropical hard woods, thus introducing these timbers into British ships. Teak soon came to be favoured for deck planking, although expensive. American ships were usually made of the woods from native coniferous trees, and this was a disadvantage as the ship aged and the open structure of these woods allowed water to soak in. British ships were copper-fastened, because the acid in oak would quickly eat into iron nails, but American ships were iron-fastened. I remember years ago in the South Seas being told that the wreck of a British ship was worth breaking down for the copper, but not so a Yankee.

In all the ships with which we are concerned, masts were made of fir. The lower masts of large ships were built up of several sectors, like a fishing rod, and the pieces held together by bands of rope at intervals. This feature appears on some good early ship models. Of course it was no longer needed when masts were of metal.

Elm wood provided protection in places subject to exposure, such as the trucks of masts, and other such cappings. Ash is suitable for oars, being springy and absorbing shocks.

Stocks of all the above woods might be held on board, and off-cuts obtainable for use in handiwork.

Oak was the common choice for the hulls of model ships, for boxes and other souvenirs of joined work, and for implements except those requiring to take heavy loads on points or thin sections. Thin and pointed tools were made of such exceptionally hard woods as ebony (plate 36), which could be obtained by the sailor ashore in tropical Africa or Asia. Lignum vitae was used for professionally made tools, but is too intractable a material for carving by hand. Small decorative objects would be made of fruitwood, and detailed carving carried out in box or hornbeam.

Knowledge of its exact material can add to the interest aroused by any object, and will often help to establish where and when it was made. The positive identification of wood requires microscopic examination of a shaving, which can be undertaken in specialist laboratories such as the Jodrell Laboratory at Kew. Without scientific tests the hardest woods are the easiest to name: the dark grainless ebony, lignum vitae with its broad streaks of lighter colour, and box, the only wood from the North temperate zone which sinks in water. If a broad, clean, untreated piece of wood is seen, the so-called 'medullary rays', appearing as bright flecks across the grain, are typical of oak.

The tool universally used by the sailor was his knife, and much genuine sailor's work will show no evidence of any other implement. This is not to say that the stock for making something round might not be

36 (left) Two fids. The larger is of ebony, marked 'H.B.M.S. Marlborough', 10in long. Probably from the 3rd rate battleship of that name, 1807–1835. The smaller fid is of cinnamon wood, length 9in, marked 'H.M. Sloop Clio', and 'John Watts 1820'. There was such a vessel at that time in reserve at Chatham

37 (centre) Head of the fid shown in plate 36, to show chip carving

38 (right) Head of the lamp-lifter shown in plate 41, to show chip carving

roughed out on a lathe by the kind offices of the ship's carpenter. The so-called 'purser's dirk' of the Royal Navy is a large clasp knife with a blunt point. It can conveniently be used for cutting rope, or chipping wood, but not for physical assault. This restriction may not these days be so necessary, but in the old Navy violence was endemic. Nor was life in the merchant navy without danger of man attacking man. The favourite 'Green River' make of seaman's knife had a point as bought, but the mates of ships would insist upon its being blunted. So chipping is typical, and an example of the detailed appearance given by this technique is shown in plate 37 and in plate 38.

Both a fid and a marline-spike are used to open up the parts of a rope for splicing but the fid is of wood, and the marline-spike of metal. The latter is of course the only tool for operating on steel-wire rope. It was, and so remains, possible to buy fids from ships' chandlers, but in the old days an able seaman might make, or at least decorate, his own. Various woods were chosen, including hickory, and ash for large fids. The use of a fid is shown in plate 39, and two specimens of old fids in plate 36.

A less usual implement made by a sailor for his own use was a serving mallet. The process of 'serving' a rope preserved it from chafing where it might rub against another rope or part of the ship. First the rope was 'wormed' with spun-yarn to fill the spiral grooves between its strands, then it was 'parcelled' with tarred canvas, and finally 'served' with spun-yarn kept taut by means of a serving mallet.

The mnemonic for the whole business was 'worm and parcel with the lay, turn and

serve the other way'. Never to be forgotten by the author since he learnt it in 1928! The *Seamanship Manual Volume I* (1926) from which I was taught has an illustration, re-drawn overleaf, which first appeared as a wood-cut in David Steel's *Elements of Seamanship* in 1794. Over the years it somehow dropped the ball of spun-yarn first shown at the loose end, which was a pity as an essential part of the work is to have a boy passing the spun-yarn ball round the rope in pace with the circulation of the mallet, on pain of many threats and curses if he goes too fast or too slow. The object shown in plate 40 is a serving 'board', the handle being in line with the working face instead

39 Harpooner using a fid to splice the foreganger to his harpoon

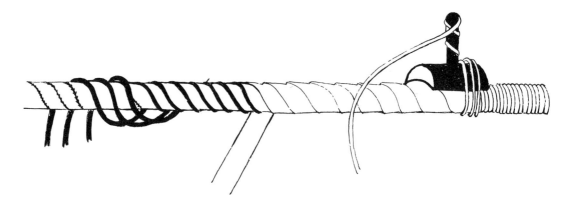

Fig 7 Parcelling a rope

40 Serving board of West Indian mahogany, length 9½in, from the Prince George, *a 2nd rate battleship built in 1772. The other side is marked 'J. Pike'*

of at right angles to it as in a mallet, but the purpose of the tool is the same.

The third implement of wood which sailors made is the rubber for smoothing the seams of sails after sewing. Kippings' *Sails and Sailmaking*, published in 1865 says 'the seams of sails must be well pressed down with a rubber'. The largest sail of a big ship would be a hundred feet or so wide, and canvas was supplied in bolts of 2ft width, so a great deal of rubbing down was required. Two rubbers are shown in plate 1. A good genuine rubber will have achieved a fine smooth patina on the working edge.

A selection of these tools of the sailors' craft may be seen in maritime museums. Best of all to my knowledge are those in the Museum of the Société Jersiaise at St Helier, collected from the old shipyards around the port.

Plate 41 shows an object which caused me some trouble to identify. The previous owner did not know what it was, but he kindly told me he had removed and discarded a hook from the bottom end, as he supposed it a later addition. However, the protruberance at the bottom end seemed to call for something to be screwed in it, so I put in a large cup-hook and started my enquiries. The first clue came from a knowledgeable retired sea officer, who said he had observed a serves to give warning of the approach of an officer on duty.

Another curious implement is illustrated in plate 42. The steel point and flat top show it to be a sail-pricker, sometimes called a 'pickwick', although that term is more properly applied to a metal-ended instrument for trimming the wicks of lamps. The sail-pricker is employed for making holes in canvas, thus a vertical thrust is all that is required. When I obtained my specimen it was roughly bound with wire over the spigot between the iron point and the boxwood body. After some thought, careful checking that the join was apparently secure, and observation that the lines

41 Lamp-lifter, probably of oak, from HMS Lyon, a 2nd rate launched in 1847. 8in high

similar thing in the wardroom of an Egyptian warship. He was told it was 'from the old times' and something to do with security. The final answer came some time later, in the museum alongside HMS *Victory* at Portsmouth. There the first comment was that such a piece had been seen aboard an old German ship, again in the wardroom. I was clearly getting 'warm', as they say, and the solution was soon reached: it is a lamp-lifter, to carry a lantern in front of the officer doing rounds of the ship in the silent hours of night.

The practical use is to avoid the burning of hands on a hot lamp, and the lifter also

Fig 8 A lamp-lifter in use

42 A sail-pricker of box wood, 7in long, probably north German, eighteenth century or earlier

suggested the point and body belonged together, I removed the wire and found the complete object was in fact quite sound. I suppose at some time it has been misused as a fid, and the wire was to strengthen against sideways forces it was never meant to withstand. The inscription was now unobscured, and I confidently expected to be able to read it, but nobody so far has been able to do this, so I reproduce it here in full.

The object has a north European air; it looks and feels old, perhaps eighteenth century or even earlier. The space between the four little columns may once have held a ball, carved from the solid as in the fork on plate 51.

The subject of sea-chests has been discussed in general terms in Chapter 1. Plate 7 shows a typical example: the brass plate on the inside of the lid, at the top near the hasps, reads 'P. Chalmers—Seaman—Dundee', which is where I obtained it, the painted ship being a square-rigger with studding-sails set, and 'Nelson chequer' on the hull. The 'ditty box' on the left side of the chest, shown in plate 8, is a compartment with a hinged lid to contain small treasures, and has been decorated in scribed work. Plate 9 shows one of the handles, made of a painted rope grommet with a leather reinforcement where it passes through the wooden piece. The chest can be dated at about 1870, chiefly by the painting of the ship, which is of Blackwall frigate tradition.

Fig 9 Inscription on the sail-pricker

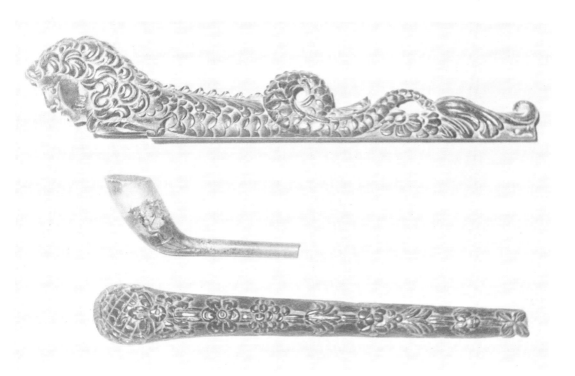

The accessories for drink and tobacco are now to be considered. The very fine and early pipe case in plate 43, of which there is a similar specimen in the Pinto Collection at Birmingham, only just qualifies for inclusion in this book, as it seems to have been made by a professional wood carver, probably a ship's carpenter used to making or repairing the 'ginger-bread' work around the sterns of ships. The style of the face, with the suggestion of a shield below it, resembles that on Dutch figure-heads, such for instance as that of Admiral De Winter's flagship at the battle of Camperdown to be seen in the grounds of Admiral Duncan's old home near Dundee. But the pipe case is considerably older than this figure-head, having for one thing no heel on the bowl of the pipe, and the material being of walnut suggests a date in the late seventeenth century.

Far removed from Dutch wood carving, but still on the subject of smoking, snuff

43 Pipe case, probably of walnut, 9¼in long, containing a contemporary clay pipe. Dutch work of the late seventeenth century

boxes in the form of coffins were popular among sailors in the last century. The origin is the slang word 'dust' for snuff, and the derived association with mortality. From this it was a small step to remember a departed friend by inscribing a coffin box with his name. The simple form of the box, with a sliding lid to keep the 'dust' in its place, would be easy enough for a sailor to make. The snuff box illustrated in plate 18 has a hinged lid, but can also be distinguished from a tobacco box by its small size. A Scottish origin is suggested by the title of the book *Psalms of David in Metre*. It is not difficult to picture the roving Scotsman who remembered his parish kirk as he took a pinch of snuff.

Proceeding from 'I snuffs' to 'I smokes'

Fig 10 A sailor and his tobacco box, from an eighteenth-century print. The inscription on the box reads 'If you loves I as I loves you, no pair so happy as we two'

and 'I chaws', a sailor's tobacco box is illustrated in plate 44, and described in the next chapter, as it is made of horn. The small size of it equates to the small size of pipes in the early days of the eighteenth century, and both are a comment on the high price of tobacco at that time. Late in that century, and early in the next, sailors' tobacco boxes became larger, and oval in shape so that they could still conveniently be carried on the

44 Tobacco box of moulded horn and wood. 3½in diameter. Dated 1712 and of that period

person. In them tobacco would be kept for smoking or for chewing. See plate 47. As to drinking, the use of coconuts for rum has been explained in Chapter 1, and plate 17 shows at the top the hole bored in the eye of the coconut. The other side of this fine nut carries the name 'Charlotte Howe' and the words:

If in St Kitts I grow on a tree so high
The negroes of the Island cut me down.
Joseph Henery did me buy. He drank my
Milk, he eat my meet, my coat he hove
away and here my body does remain until
This very day.

A very similar sentimental rhyme, in this case supposed to be spoken by the tree from which it was cut in 'Otaheite', that is Tahiti, is carved on a cudgel dated 1828, giving the name of HMS *Seringapatam*. This ship was a 5th rate of 46 guns, built in 1819, not to be confused with the Blackwall Frigate of that name mentioned later in this chapter.

The nut shown in plate 45 is more crudely done. The panels not shown depict 'A Lady taking the Air', 'A Lt. of Marines' and 'A Serg. of Marines'. The crowded decoration, not to mention the Captain's umbrella, suggest an early nineteenth-century date.

The last of these coconuts illustrated was

45 (left) Inscribed coconut. Major axis 5½in. Early nineteenth century

46 (right) Drinking cup made from a coconut. The other side is carved with an Irish harp. Original major axis 5in. Mid-nineteenth century

equipped with a cover, no doubt made from the missing part of it, evidenced by two holes under the rim for its attachment. The side not shown in plate 46 is inscribed with an Irish harp and 'Erin Go Brach'. The ship appears to be a merchantman of perhaps about 1840. Notice the flag of St Patrick, flying sturdily against the wind.

Of course not all carved coconuts are the work of sailors. Some can be found decorated in South America with various emblems, such as eagles, and other nuts have geometric designs and are difficult to place. The 'eyes' of the coconut are often shown with two out of three as eyes, the other as a mouth, the assembly being a human face. It is an old tradition among the Polynesians that a coconut will not fall on you, as it has eyes and can see where it is going.

Quite a different nut is shown in plate 48. Here is an 'ivory nut', providing a material known as vegetable ivory, and used last century for small objects such as buttons. The source of the nut is a South American palm, and the iron barque *Peruvian*, homeward bound with a cargo of these nuts, did not survive being driven ashore at Seaford.

The final class of wooden objects to be discussed, other than models of ships and boats, are those things of no particularly marine context. A walking stick, indeed, is little used aboard ship, but plate 49 shows a fine one, made of ebony from Macassar and inlaid with pearl-shell, in a manner reminiscent of Maori work. These materials, together with the competent workmanship, manrope knot handle, the stick spiralled to suggest a narwhal tusk, add up to it having been made in the middle of last century aboard a whaling ship, quite probably American, in the Pacific. These scrimshaw sticks (see also plate 50) have the head spigotted on. I have seen forlorn examples with the head having been lost. It would be

When I took Peg Block, in tow, Splinter my Mizzen if I want fool enough to swear by my Honor, to stick to her as long as she had a plank left, or I'd given her turnips before now but if a man forfeits his Honor, de ye mind me; he's not worth a fiddler's D—n.

Why now de'see Jack, as how thus here's my way of thinking when a man takes a girl under his protection, she should be all as one as a piece of his self, and she should share his last farthing

SATURDAY NIGHT at SEA or Nautica

60

y what now de'See's the use of all this here sort
'luff' about Honor and all that there: if a
ans a man he'l allways do whats right, and if
he is no Man, my Eyes and limbs throw him
over board, that theres my way o'thinking D—ne

Why that theres what I was a saying to
that there Yorkshireman, you know who
I mean Tom Starboards messmate, they
call him Isaac Scarlet;— the Da—n'd
lubber took poor Ann under his protec-
-tion as he call it, and made the poor
creature pawn her Necklace, and all
them there things to get him
grogg and such like D—n
such sort of Honor!!

London Pub. by S.W.Fores 50 Piccadilly & 312 Oxford Street.

s of Honor.

difficult to replace such an important part to restore the stick satisfactorily.

The group of things shown in plate 51 might, except for their history and the anchor motif on the spoon, have been made by landsmen, the spoon and fork by Welsh lads for their sweethearts and the knitting stick in the north of England.

The pin-cushion in the form of a bellows (plate 52) is marked in dots of paint 'Royal George Sunk 1782', with some initials and a cross. This year was indeed the date when that ship, while being heeled to expose the side for repairs to a sea-cock, suddenly broke up and foundered. The findings of·the subsequent court martial were not made public at the time, for they revealed certain grave faults in the construction and maintenance of HM ships. The pin-cushion seems to be a contemporary 'memento mori', but the initials do not fit the names of any person known to me to have been lost in the sinking.

The knitting stick shown in plate 53 is a north country device, which was adopted by the Brixham fisher-folk who migrated each summer to such northern parts as Scarborough for seasonal trawling in nearby waters. The stick is held at the left of the waist hooked over a belt called a cow-band. A needle projecting from the top of this stick left a hand free to manipulate the wool with increased speed than without the stick. I have never seen a specimen with the needle remaining in it, but the hole for it should of course be observable.

In the eighteenth century another purely domestic accessory was made and decorated in north Germany and Denmark. These so-called mangle-boards are similar to a modern ironing board, but smaller, and would, I suppose, have been used chiefly on sleeves, to shape them after washing. Their style of decoration has led them to be

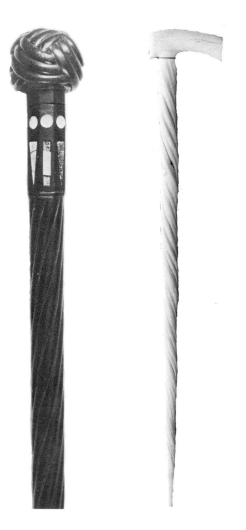

48 (above) Pen drawing of the wreck of the Peruvian *at Seaford, Sussex, on a nut of vegetable ivory. The* Peruvian *was an iron barque built in 1875. Major diameter of the nut 3in*

49 (centre) Walking stick of Macassar ebony, with pearl shell inlay, the head carved with a manrope knot and the shaft to simulate a narwhal tusk. Whaling ship work of about 1840

50 (right) Stick of narwhal tusk, the head carved from a sperm whale tooth. Length 3ft. Late nineteenth century

considered as sailors' work, but this theory has never been demonstrated satisfactorily to me.

Before describing the models of ships and boats made by sailors, let us first consider models of other kinds. These were made to assist in the design and construction of ships, to display their features and advertise them, or models were made with the prime purpose of actual sailing.

The typical shipbuilder's model is a severely practical-looking solid half-hull attached to a board. Positions for the masts and bowsprit may be indicated, but decor-

ation is absent, for this is perhaps one of a series of 'maquettes', as a sculptor might call them, to be modified and perhaps discarded until a design is reached worthy to form the basis of a ship's plans. At that stage the lines of the proposed ship can be lifted by shaping lead wire to the model. A more sophisticated way is to cut the model vertically or transversely thus obtaining slices from which the body and sheer plans can be drawn. This is no place for an essay on ship construction, but I mention these technicalities because shipbuilders' models can be found made in slices pinned together.

The model shown in plate 30 will serve as a bridge between the shipbuilder's model, concerned with design, and the dockyard model, concerned with translation of design into actuality. The *Seringapatam* model is clearly in the second of these groups, but the framing and planking of the hull is what matters, so masts and other details are only briefly indicated. Notice the stout and close-set timbers, and the absence of sheer typical of the early Blackwall frigate.

A true dockyard model will show every detail in miniature. Although chiefly made for advertisement—using the word in its broadest sense—they could be of practical use in such matters as demonstrating how machinery can or cannot be removed for repair, the flow of passengers coming aboard, or the stowage of cargo. Dockyard models from the seventeenth century to modern times may be seen in the National Maritime Museum at Greenwich and a superb assembly of British Navy Board models crossed the Atlantic just before World War I to find a home in the United States of America at Annapolis. These were the models made in

51 (left) Love spoon, love fork and knitting sheath, of various woods, from the Pinto Collection, all reputedly sailor made. The sheath is inlaid with sealing wax. The spoon is 9in long

52 (right) A pin cushion in the form of a bellows, marked 'Royal George Sunk 1782' made of a dark hardwood, perhaps mahogany, and 4¼in long

53 Knitting sheath, probably of beech. Nine-teenth century

His Majesty's dockyards to show to Government officials, such as Samuel Pepys, to Naval officers, and to Royalty itself. They were accurate miniatures of the real thing, except that it was usual to omit the planking below the water line in order to show the interior construction of the hull. The normal scale was 1:48, so that every inch of the model equalled 4ft of the ship.

Ship models made as practical sailers have their own special features. The hull will almost certainly be weighted, the sail plan will probably be simplified, by the omission of stay sails for instance, gaffs and booms will be secured by eyelets to the mast, and the running rigging may use a special sort of bead instead of properly made blocks, for ease of running the little lines through them. In brief, accuracy must give way to practical requirements. Of course these models are excellent in their way. I remember before World War II there was a group of enthusiasts at Lymington who used to sail their model boats on the salterns every Sunday after church. Blue blazers and peaked caps were worn, and it was quite an occasion.

There is a class of ship models made for no practical purpose, unlike those already described, but which must be distinguished if possible from those made by sailors in their leisure. I refer to the work of French prisoners-of-war in England at the time of the Napoleonic Wars. These men, during their

incarceration aboard hulks in the Thames, or in prisons, were allowed to supplement their resources by the sale of whatever they could make from the materials available to them. With skill and ingenuity they used the bones from their food, small pieces of wood, straw, even their own hair, to make and rig ship models which now command very high prices. The tradition of fine carving existed in France, notably in Dieppe. It is the high standard of prisoner-of-war work, and the bones from meat used in it, that distinguish their ship models from sailors' handicraft.

Now I will mention the well-known ships in bottles, but only to dismiss them. Although a few of these have some interest and even artistic merit, the ship in a bottle exists chiefly to cause the unsophisticated to ask how it got there. The 'model' is generally a flimsy affair not representing any particular vessel, and the rigging is disposed only to hold the masts upright. A good small ship model will be all the better if it does not have to be folded up to pass through the neck of a bottle. I have also seen a model of the Crucifixion, made of bone, in a bottle. There were three crosses, the cross-bars hinged to the upright, and the instruments of the Passion had also been inserted.

The classes of ship models which are not the concern of this book have now been eliminated and it remains to consider those which are. The indications of an old sailor-made ship model are various. All may not be present in every model, but sufficient to

HERRING DRIFTER
Marmion of Yarmouth

54 Model of a Yarmouth herring drifter with lugger rig, about 1860, length overall 18in

form a consensus. Considerable attention is paid to the details of the rigging, with threads of different sizes in appropriate positions. The sails are either furled, or not set at all. The general use of wood is typical, the hull being solid and somewhat roughly made, the masts and yards often too thick for accuracy. The paint may be thick and tarry, being in fact the tailings of such pots as the ship's painter could spare. Full models are often cased (plate 4), with a painted background and a painted wood 'sea', which is cut to receive the model at floating level. A model formerly in my possession was secured in the 'sea' by two long pins driven through the hull just below it. I have seen models no longer thus cased with holes through the hull, now plugged and painted over, which could have been used for this method of fixing.

It is roughly true to say that the later the model the more accurately it is made, sometimes at the expense of its spirit as a work of art.

There is in Brixham Museum an interesting

model of the topsail schooner *Helen*, built in 1820 and out of Lloyd's Register in 1867. If the model was made between these dates, it is unusually finely constructed. The *Helen* was a Brixham vessel, and the model has every appearance of considerable age: my conclusion is that it was made about a hundred years ago, as a souvenir of the ship. In the collection at the United States Naval Academy at Annapolis there is a model similar to those shown in plates 38 and 39, with the same doll-like figure-head and indications of gold scrolling on the beak-head. The model at Annapolis is catalogued as 'the work of an amateur'.

I have toyed with the idea that models made on the east coast of Britain have certain special characteristics. Certainly I have only seen the full-hull model set in a painted sea, with a painted back-board, from east coast ports; but to make any definite pronouncement would need very considerable

55 *Model of the Dundee whaler* Narwhal, *one of the whaling fleet from that port. This is a contemporary model, length 40in overall. The* Narwhal *was built in 1859, and lost in the Davis Straits in 1884*

research, and it must remain for the moment an open question.

A very attractive group consists of those half-hull models set in deep cases, the sails carved of wood and the sea commonly of painted plaster as in plates 32 and 56. The fashion for making them appears to have been short-lived, around the middle of the nineteenth century. Perhaps the best I ever saw was recently on the London market, at a high price. It was small, and simply but carefully made, the sea in this instance being of wood sawn with diagonal cuts to shape triangular waves. The name 'Robert and Sarah' was painted on a little pediment above the opening of the case, and Lloyd's Register gives a snow of that name built at Sunderland in 1854, and stranded in 1869.

56 Half-hull models of a ship and a schooner.
About 1860. Length of case 3½ft. The ship is
of Blackwall frigate type, and flies the appropriate house-flag

57 Model of a whale-boat. Probably the work
of a ship's carpenter, late nineteenth century,
and made of walnut. Length overall 20in

The rig of a snow is similar to a brig, but the driver is on a separate mizzen mast, and this feature was shown in the model, adding to its interest and authenticity.

Models of sailing ships are not the only ones encountered. I have seen a model of the British submarine C3, one of a class built just before World War I, and the last to have petrol engines. Later submarines had diesel engines. This model seemed to be a contemporary one, the hull of solid wood and the external details as, for instance, the conning tower of thin gauge metal such as would have been available on board the submarine itself. It was about 15in long.

Models of boats which can reasonably be claimed as the work of sailors are rare. The whale boat illustrated in plate 57, which I bought in Salisbury some years ago and gave to the Dundee Museum, has its sides properly planked up and is probably the work of a carpenter.

The question whether a model was made by a sailor cannot be answered with certainty unless there is documentary evidence. A small model made of hand-worked simple materials is more likely to be shipboard work than a larger more sophisticated specimen. Examination of known genuine models will soon give a feeling for the truth of them and, unlike the 'Sunday painter' type of marine picture, they are not easy to fake.

This book does not deal with paintings, but I will mention here that oil paintings of ships, in a folk art style, were certainly done in the old days, but the majority of those on sale today are modern reproductions. Examination of the back of the picture will reveal the endeavours made to 'antique' the frame and the panel, or canvas.

5
BONE, IVORY, HORN
AND SHELLS

Because the word 'scrimshaw' is most frequently used about carved and inscribed objects of ivory and bone, this is the best place to attempt a definition of it. Barrière and Leland in their *Dictionary of Slang* (1897) give 'scrimshaw' and 'scrimshandy' as synonymous, said to be an Americanism meaning 'anything made by sailors for themselves in their leisure hours'. This book also has an entry under 'scrimshanker', as an army expression for one who avoids foreign service, or malingers to escape duty. It gives the origin of this as 'scrimp', 'to shorten' ('skimp' must be the same) and 'swanker', 'to labour'. Mayhew and Skeat's *Dictionary of Middle English* gives 'swinken' as 'to toil'. It seems therefore that our word 'scrimshaw' was originally used in a perjorative sense, but became respectable. It is indeed known that whaling captains encouraged their crew to employ their spare time on scrimshaw, no doubt reflecting that Satan would otherwise find work for idle hands. The modern accepted spelling of the word seems to be through confusion with the surname Scrimshaw. The first literary reference to scrimshaw as a handicraft is in 1828, in the ship's log of an American whaler, and my own definition of the word would be 'anything made for themselves by the sailors of ocean-going whaling ships, in the nineteenth and early twentieth centuries, during their leisure hours'.

Both opportunity and official encouragement combined to develop an extensive folk art among whalers' crews. There was spare time in passage to and from the whaling grounds, and many hours waiting for the cry of 'there she blows'. The officers would permit the ship's artizans to assist in the provision of files, chisels, gimlets, jig-saws, even lathes, to work the by-products of whaling—bone, teeth, and baleen—into all manner of things. Work of good quality was achieved, and an extensive repertoire of motifs were engraved. The invocation 'greasy luck to . . .' is often seen, and the common emblems of the tattoo artist are freely used (plate 10). If a woman was to be portrayed, her fashionable dress might be copied from *Godey's Lady's Book* (plates 33 and 34) in the USA, or *The Englishwoman's Domestic Magazine*, a similar publication in Great Britain.

Of all the things made and decorated by sailors, those by ivory and bone from the old whaling ships are the most attractive and sought after by collectors. Whole books have been written about scrimshaw, and it is not my purpose to follow with another volume, but only to provide an outline of the subject.

In the seventeenth century whaling voyages were made to hunt the Greenland right whale in northern waters. The Dutch were first in the field, led there in search of the North East passage to China, and the

British followed. Early in the nineteenth century these whaling fleets worked their way westward into the Davis Straits and Baffin Bay as whales became scarce in nearer waters. The outbreak of World War I put an end to northern whaling, and by then the quarry had been so reduced in numbers as to be in danger of extinction. The right whale or 'bowhead', as whaling men called it, was the more important commercially of the two large whales of the family Balaenidae, namely the Greenland and the Biscay right whales. The word 'right whale' apparently simply means a whale worth catching, for these creatures provided large quantities of oil, and also 'baleen', which occurs as an extensive series of hard, horny, triangular plates growing from the roof of the mouth. This 'whalebone', a term I will not use again, to avoid confusion with the real bone of the whale, was used in women's stays, to make brushes and such things. It commanded its highest price in 1870.

At the risk of over-simplification, it may be said that the right whales were the quarry of European whaling men, and the sperm whales the prey of American whalers. The baleen whales are peaceful animals, content to browse on 'krill', a shrimp-like creature abounding near the surface in their home waters, by taking in mouthfuls and sifting the krill through their great baleen sieves. The sperm whale or cachalot is quite different. He belongs to the sub-order Odontoceti, the toothed whales, and is equipped with formidable teeth to bite the squids on which he feeds into gulpable portions. These teeth can be used to good effect against his pursuers, for which see plate 15. There are forty-two teeth in the lower jaw of this sort of whale, and the largest of them can be up to 8in or so in length. The sperm whale is a wanderer, found in all oceans, but migrating to warmer waters as the winter comes to the northern or the southern seas.

Back in the seventeenth century the inhabitants of New England took to off-shore whaling. The weather vane on the house of a friend of mine in East Hampton, reputed the seventeenth oldest house in the USA, is in the form of a sperm whale, dated 1683. A hundred years later the first American whalers entered the Pacific, and started a tradition of ocean voyages after the whale which were to continue until the early years of this century. Voyages of four or five years were not unusual, from the home port in New England to the 'coasts of Peru, where the sperm whales blow', then whaling and rendering down the blubber on board until tanks were full, finally the long slog back, and the share-out of the proceeds in agreed proportions. The story of Moby Dick, who was of course a sperm whale, and the film of it made by Orson Welles, recapture life aboard one of the old 'spouters'. Captain Ahab speaks of Moby Dick as 'all the sin and sorrow of this world', and their relation is lifted above that of whaler and whale; it is St George and the Dragon; Marduk and Tiamat. My only personal experience of a whale concerns one called Molly, who visited False Bay in South Africa, sometimes with her latest calf, for some years in succession during World War II. On one occasion she entered Simonstown Harbour when the boom was opened to admit a ship, and became much alarmed to find the boom closed against her. Cruising round the harbour, she surfaced to blow, and a friend of mine was unlucky enough to be down wind. He told me that the odour of a whale's breath must be experienced; it is quite indescribable.

Plate 57 shows a whale-boat of those days.

70

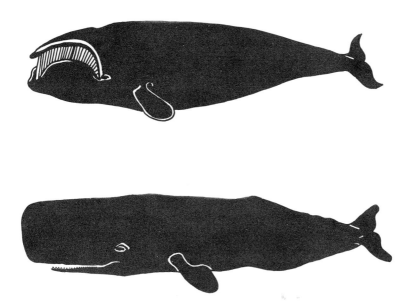

The post in the stern is called a logger-head. The line was coiled in a tub between the after thwarts, and turns were taken round the logger-head when the harpoon had been successfully lodged in a whale. The line then ran forwards and through chocks in the boat's stem. The whale-boat had a crew of six, including the boat-steerer who pulled the bow oar and threw the harpoon, then changed places with the boat-header, who had been steering the boat with an oar over the stern. It was the boat-header who finally killed the exhausted whale with a lance. It was a cruel business, but the men who did it faced danger with bravery, and could have had no understanding of the pain they were inflicting on a particularly intelligent animal.

Whaling ships were of wood, the early ones ship-rigged, with some barques and brigs later (see plate 19). Auxiliary steam was eagerly adopted, for use in calms or to claw away from lee shores. The American custom was for the look-out to stand in a hoop at the foretop; in British whalers the comfort of a barrel was provided. But no general con-

Fig 11 (above) a right whale; (below) a sperm whale

clusions can be drawn from this. I have seen a jack-stay transfer between British and American ships in which a British officer was hauled over, suspended with only his feet in a wire loop, but the American travelled in what looked like a Sedan chair.

The two sorts of whale are easily distinguished (See Figure 11 above).

The 'blowing' can be identified by experienced whaling men, the sperm whale having a single blow-hole at the end of the snout, and the right whale having two blow-holes.

The teeth from toothed whales, the baleen from whalebone whales, and the bones from both were available to the crews of whaling ships. It was the privilege of the mate in charge of the flensing deck to allocate among the crew the sperm whale teeth, these being highly prized for scrimshaw but having no commercial value. Pieces of bone were freely available, and the dense ivory-like bone of the sperm whale's jaw was preferred. Baleen having a commercial use, only off-cuts

71

would generally find their way below. See plates 58 and 59.

Let us leave the unpleasant and extremely smelly environs of the whaler's deck, and suppose ourselves the happy owner of a sperm whale's tooth. It has been sawn through above the root, is 5in long, and has a rough ribbed surface. The first task is to file and polish the tooth, using sand first and finishing with ash from under the ship's try-pot. It all takes time, but the work must be completed while the tooth is fresh, so that a final soaking in brine will leave a surface temporarily soft enough to be engraved with flowing lines having some variation in depth. Designs would also be engraved in stipple, perhaps through a fashion plate or other picture on paper, pasted to the tooth and subsequently washed off. Whether lines or dots, a darkening was given to the completed design with ink, soot or tobacco juice, red ink being sometimes used as well as the more normal black. A final polish was then given with wood-ash.

I have described this process and its result because engraving, especially on sperm whale teeth, is extensively practised these days, sometimes as reproductions not intended to pass as old (plate 60), but all too

58 A baleen busk, inscribed in needlepoint with ships and an unidentified harbour scene. Length 14½in. Early nineteenth century

59 Detail of inscribed drawing on busk in plate 58. Note the flush deck of the battleship on the left, which is a late feature

often as deliberate fakes, as in plate 61. If you find a scrimshaw tooth with a jagged base, or an industriously rounded one, the surface perhaps scratched and the scratches filled with dirt, beware! It may be a genuine article which has fallen on hard times, but is more likely to be a fake, particularly if the surface where the decoration has been done appears to be in better condition than the surrounding areas. Again, if under a magnifying glass the inscribed lines appear jumpy and jagged, this may be old work badly done, but is more likely to be the result of recent failure to prepare the tooth properly. Finally, the subject matter of reproduction scrimshaw may well be superficially attractive, whether it be a simpering maiden or an effusive goddess. The sperm whale is still hunted, and the teeth are brought back. Not only are there new teeth available but the carcases of whales may be

Fig 12 *An illustration in* Costume through the Ages, *from a picture by Downham, depicting eighteenth-century dress*

60 *(right) Sperm whale tooth, decorated with an engraving taken from* Costume through the Ages, *a book published in 1964. 6in high without the stand*

61 *(below) Engraved sperm whale tooth, length 4in. A modern reproduction*

62 (left) Sperm whale tooth engraved with the figure of a girl in South American dress. Collected in Peru in the 1890s and work of that period. Length 5½in

63 (centre) Sperm whale tooth decorated in stipple, known to have belonged to a whaling Captain. Date of the costume about 1855. Height 6in

64 (right) Sperm whale tooth engraved with a sailor, having 'Cornelia' on his shirt. HMS Cornelia was the captured slaver Venus, taken off Calabar in 1828 and this tooth was engraved in stipple about 1835. Height 5in

washed ashore. I know that recently the skeleton of a sperm whale was discovered in a remote bay of the Falkland Islands, and the teeth were removed. So even carbon dating would not ensure that the work was old.

The situation is such that some dealers will not risk their reputations by dealing in scrimshaw. Quite recently whaling men have carved sperm whale teeth into the semblance of penguins and other creatures. A pleasing hobby, but I do not find these things attractive.

The bright side of all this doubt and deception is that fully authenticated scrimshaw teeth do exist, and a pair of them are illustrated in plates 62 and 63, together with a selection of others which are almost certainly all that they appear to be.

I have dealt at some length with sperm whale tooth scrimshaw, because it is both typical and pre-eminent. Decoration was however also practised on walrus tusks (plate 66), even on elephant and hippopotamus tusks. I have heard of a complete walrus skull decorated in scrimshaw: no

65 (left) Sperm whale tooth, engraved about 1850. 6in high without stand

66 (right) Two walrus tusks engraved probably in the late nineteenth century. 16in high without stand

doubt a great rarity, but most unlovely with little doubt. The walrus was hunted by eskimos, and their tusks obtained from them by trade or barter in northern waters. These beasts grow to a prodigious size, and the record length of a tusk from one of them is over 3ft long, so that it might be mistaken for the tusk of an elephant. Without plenty of experience it is not possible to distinguish the ivory from different creatures. Walrus ivory is said to be more silky in feel than elephant, but this distinction is not apparent to me. I have, however, noticed that the grain of elephant ivory shows up well, whereas walrus ivory seems without grain but has length-wise areas of cloudy appearance, less dense in colour than the remainder. An uncut walrus tusk is at once identified by its oval section, pronounced near the tip. Plate 67 shows specimens of these two materials: the grain of the elephant ivory can just be distinguished in the photograph; on the snuff bottle itself it is more evident.

The special product of the right whale, its baleen, was used to make busks, described by the *Century Dictionary* as 'flexible strips

67 (left) Snuff bottle of elephant ivory and fid of walrus ivory, for comparison of materials

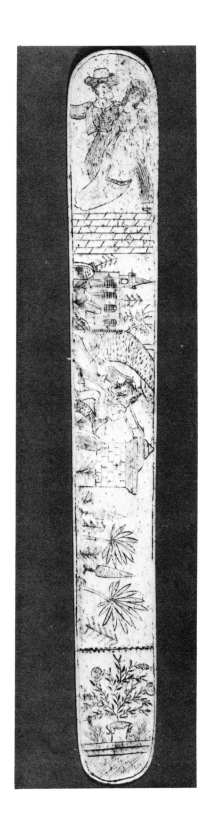

68 (right) A busk of whale bone. The style (compare with plate 66) and the wide hat of the sailor, suggests a late nineteenth-century date, when busks were no longer worn, but they may still have been given as love tokens. Length 12in

of wood, steel, whalebone, or other stiffening material, placed in the front of stays to keep them in form'. These instruments of correction were used in the late eighteenth and early nineteenth centuries, fitted into a sheath down the front of the stays. See plates 58, 59 and 68. Both of these could conceivably be worn, but I have seen busks of carved wood so large as surely to be

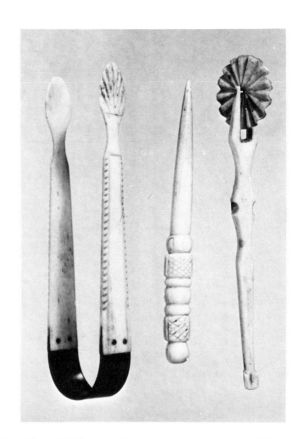

impracticable, and which may be regarded only as tokens of love.

The notable difference between bone and ivory is that bone remains a living material within the living body. It grows and can heal after breaking, for which purpose it is provided with numerous small canals. These under favourable conditions will show up as black specks on the cut surface of the bone, as in plate 68. Ivory has no such canals, but a grain similar to wood can sometimes be seen, as in plate 69, particularly in elephant ivory, as already discussed.

The bone of whales has no special virtue over that of other animals, but it was readily available and therefore used to make a variety of objects, mostly for domestic use. The most spectacular are the wool-winders, which open up on lazy tongs to provide a

69 (left) Ivory pipe stopper, engraved with a sperm whale and initials. 2½in high. Made about 1850

70 (right) Three minor items of scrimshaw. Sugar tongs (length 6in), bodkin, and pie-crimper. All of whale bone, and nineteenth century

drum of criss-crossing whale-bone staves for the holding of a skein of wool to be made into balls. The sewing box illustrated in plate 6 is a fine example of work in whalebone. The maker has carved strips of pan-bone to achieve a rustic effect. The interior partitions of the box appear to be professional work.

A selection of the less important scrimshaw made of whalebone is shown in plates 69 to 73. The tortoise-shell spring of the sugar tongs in plate 70 is very neatly

77

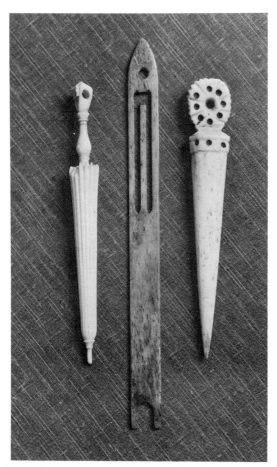

scarfed into the bone of the 'spoons', and the style of the tongs suggests a silver original of early nineteenth-century date. The pie-crimper was rather a favourite thing for whaling men to make, perhaps reminding them of past home cooking and looking forward to a happy return. The middle object in plate 71 is a braiding needle. It is thin and accurately flat: the surface is smoothed and stained by use with tarred twine. I cannot say of what bone it is made. These braiding needles held a small amount of twine, by looping over the interior pin near the top, round the indent at the bottom, up and around the pin the other side, and so on. The use was for repairing large nets, or making small ones—rabbit nets for instance.

71 (left) Needle-case, braiding needle (length 8in), and bodkin. The needle-case and bodkin of whale bone, the braiding needle probably of ox bone, and fisherman's work. Nineteenth century, or early twentieth century

72 (below) Toddy ladle of whale bone. Late nineteenth century. Length 8in

They are therefore not specifically for whaling, nor indeed exclusively marine. I believe the illustrated specimen was made and used by a fisherman. The right-hand object on the same plate is claimed as a bodkin, that is to say an object used for threading ribbon into clothes and such-like, because of the hole at its top end. The spike shown in plate 71 is probably also for use on garments, but it might be a small fid, for decorative rope-work. The toddy ladle in plate 72 would hopefully be used with a footed toddy bowl containing spirits with sugar and hot water, a favourite tipple among the Scots. I once owned a toddy bowl of china, with the legend 'Success to the William of Dundee', dated 1847, specially decorated to celebrate the launching of that ship.

A highly-prized material for walking sticks is the tusk of the narwhal, which is distinguished among other sea mammals by the male beast having one long horn, twisted along its length and elegantly tapered. In the Middle Ages narwhal tusks were accepted to be the horns of unicorns, and greatly valued. There was a narwhal tusk displayed beside the 'Lady and Unicorn' tapestries in the Musée de Cluny, in Paris. No explanation was given, but the significance was clear and indeed the unicorn in the tapestry, kneeling by the maiden, has a long horn like the tusk in appearance. Plate 50 shows one of these tusks as a walking stick, and plate 49 shows a stick of wood with the shaft similarly spiralled.

We have now dealt enough with scrimshaw, as defined at the beginning of this chapter, and turn to other things of animal origin. First there is the splendid cow's horn shown in plates 74 and 75, skilfully engraved with a view of the departure of the British Fleet from Havana, when Cuba was restored to Spain by the Treaty of Paris. The name James Scott, with a heraldically defective coat of arms and the motto 'Dread God'

73 Umbrella with handle and rib ferrules of whale bone, the ribs themselves of baleen. Length 3in. About 1890

74 *Cow's horn, inscribed with the departure of the British Fleet from Havana on July 7th 1763, when Cuba was restored to Spain by the Treaty of Paris. Length 12in. Contemporary work*

75 *Another view of the 'Havana' cow's horn*

appears on the horn but is not seen in the plates. There is no family with the name Scott who are recorded as bearing the 'ordinary' depicted, a 'stag's head erased', or the motto. There is no James Scott named in the recent book *Cuba* by Hugh Thomas,

in connection with the capture and restoration of Havana, or in the *Dictionary of National Biography* or *American Biography*. My conclusion is that the engraving may have been done by a master's mate or other junior officer in the Fleet. The representation of the port and its fortifications suggest the work of someone acquainted with the art of navigation. It is interesting to note that Salford, where the horn now is, was the port for off-loading West Indian cotton to feed the looms of Lancashire.

The first chapter of this book told about the sailor's fondness for tobacco, and plate 44

76 Trochus shell engraved with a view of the Great Eastern, *dated 1858 and work of that period. 3½in high*

shows a baccy box, with a similar sentiment on it to the later box shown in Figure 10.

Tobacco boxes of moulded horn sides and wood top and base were popular in the early days of smoking, certainly in the seventeenth century, but larger and more substantial boxes came to be used later, as is shown in plate 44. As with many other handicrafts, sailors' work can only be positively identified by its known history.

Shell is an intractable material for handiwork, but it is readily available to the sailor and he has sometimes decorated it. The trochus shell in plate 76 has been sanded and polished to show the nacre, then engraved. The huge *Great Eastern*, built by I. K. Brunel technically in advance of her time, succeeded only in laying the Atlantic cable, and was never a success on the regular run to the United States, for which she was intended. The flat surface of the tropical pearl oyster, which also provides the commercial mother of pearl, can be decorated, and I have seen one with a compass on it which might confidently be ascribed the work of a sailor.

6

CORDAGE AND TEXTILES

This chapter concerns the decorative uses to which vegetable and animal fibres, spun or woven, have been put by sailors. Progressing upwards from the simplest work, let us start with knotting, which is also used in the course of a seaman's employment; moving to the subtleties of sennit, macramé and drawn thread work; finally to consider wool pictures and other embroidery. Clearly one does not have to be a sailor to make these things, but as with ships' models the motifs and styles will often establish a nautical origin beyond reasonable doubt. Moreover the seafaring man has perforce to ply his own needle, in the absence of female assistance, and it is a small step from darning socks to working wool pictures. I remember in particular one very burly naval officer, a champion swimmer and well-known rugger player, whose relaxation was knitting, which he did supremely well.

First of all, then, we have knots, that is to say rope or any other material of round section tied together. A reef knot is plain and useful, but when we progress up the scale of complexity to the star knot (plate 77), here is a practical way of securing a rope so that it will not pass through a ring, but also an object of some beauty. From this point onwards there is no limit to ingenuity, and in specialist books on knotting will be found fanciful pieces of no practical use but of fine quality, comparable to other artistic creations. I have confined my illustrations (plates 77 to 79) to a series of knots which

may serve good purpose with elegance, and I have added plate 80, to show that complex knotting for a utilitarian purpose is not yet extinct.

Old decorative and specimen knots may be found in the antique shops of seaport towns, often made from the small hemp and cotton line which was supplied primarily for cod or mackerel fishing. A Naval origin will be betrayed if a coloured jute thread has been worked into hemp rope: blue for Portsmouth dockyard, red for Devonport, and yellow for Chatham. This is the 'rogues yarn', to deter peculation of government stores. Nowadays the preferred material for fancy knots is nylon (plate 79) which personally I find harsh and unattractive. It is, however, easy to work and, like other plastic products, not subject to natural decay.

Examples of old knots are encountered laid out on knot boards, for the instruction of boys, cadets, or apprentices, as in plate 81. These boards may be simple flat affairs, or framed, or made to fold like a travelling chess board. If in original condition they can be of interest to show regional differences in the practice of knotting. I remember a discussion around the knot boards in the Naval Museum at Istanbul between naval officers from many countries. It was established that the same knots are used for the same purposes through Europe and America, but there are minor differences. A detailed study would indicate the routes by which nautical knowledge has been diffused.

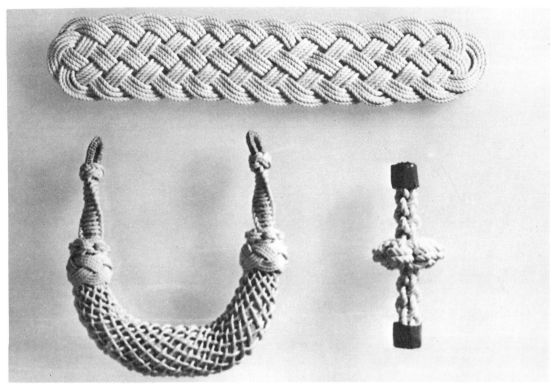

77 (top) Six head plaited mat, single strand 'doubled' twice

(left) Rope handle for sea chest. Ringbolt hitching forming eyes. Turks head decoration followed by banister bars and six-strand star knot

(right) Star knot, with six-strand round sennit forming shroud. All modern

78 (left) Stanchion covering of Turks head lashing. Terminal constructed of eight-strand diamond knots, doubled

(middle) 'Chinese' lanyard with three part Turks head on core terminal

(right) Bell pull of six strands. Becket and six-strand sennit forming the eye. Twelve-strand Matthew Walker knot followed by twelve-strand star knot with strengthening. Two by one diamond covering with diamond knot to lock. Single-strand monkey's fist ball terminal. All modern

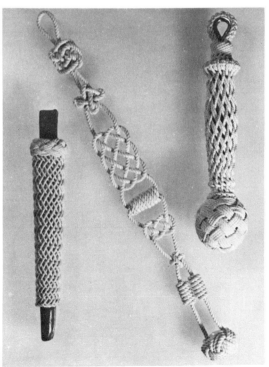

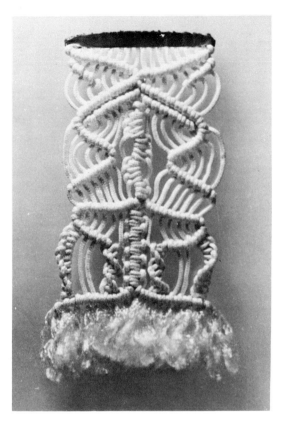

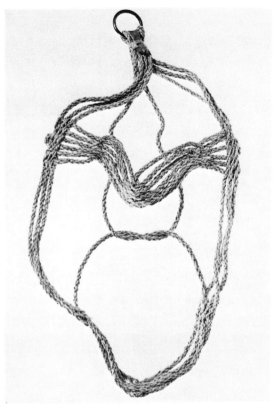

79 (left) A short section of macramé. Modern

80 (right) Donkey's bridle worked from hemp cord. Bought in Turkey, 1972. Length extended 1ft 10in

Sennit, already encountered while discussing sailors' hats in Chapter 3, is plaiting, as distinct from the tying-together process of knotting. An early definition is given in that excellent work *Boteler's Dialogues*, published in 1634, which says it is 'line or string composed of rope yarn; and for the most part consisteth of 3, 6 or 9 strings divided into 3 parts, and then plaited one over another, and beaten small and flat, with a mallet of wood'. This form of sennit would have been kept handy for various purposes: perhaps to make up a mat, or to prevent

spars and other woodwork from chafing together. If sennit is made from four parts instead of three, it turns out square in section, and this square sennit was used for piston packing in the old low-pressure steam-reciprocating engines. Another special use of sennit was for log lines, connecting the impeller towed behind the ship with the indicator fixed on the stern rails. The advantage here is that sennit is not liable to kink, as is rope.

Macramé is a special kind of knotting, worked in a number of cords suspended from a bar or a line, or it may be formed out of a fringe of cords combed from the cut edge of a woven material. I believe that the origin of the word may be traced to the knotting of a fringe, because I have seen hand towels in Turkey thus treated, and the word 'makrama'

Fig 13 Sailor with sennit hat

is old Turkish for a towel, taken from the Arabic. The technique of macramé is well suited to ornamenting the edges of canopies, for example over the stern sheets of boats, and its nautical use may date back to the days of the Levant Company. Ladies in the reign of Queen Victoria found macramé an agreeable hobby, and it has recently enjoyed a considerable revival in the making of shawls, even clothes.

The exceptional example of macramé work shown in plate 82 was perhaps made for use in a boat, to shade a square port, or screen a ledge. Otherwise it may have been just an example of the maker's virtuosity. Although its full history is not known, it came from a maritime environment and has every appearance of being a sailor's work. Plate 79 shows a piece of modern macramé, suitable for edging the canopy of a boat.

81 A knot board, with examples of various knots and sennits. Recent work

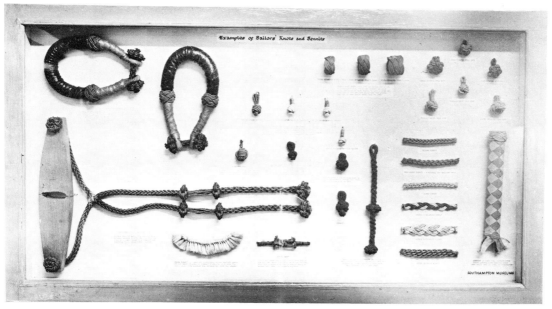

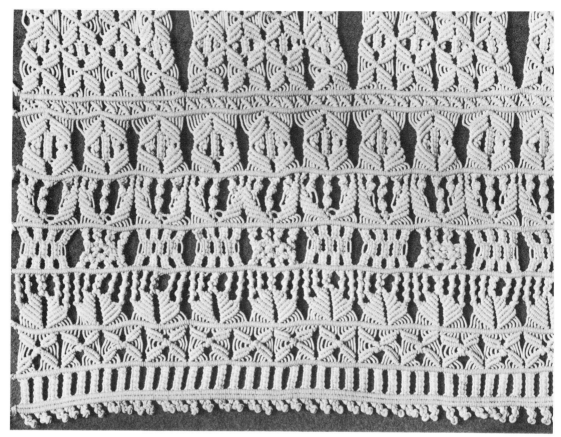

82 Macramé work in cotton line, probably nineteenth century. The piece is 10in deep

The sailor can readily turn his hand to the practice of needlework, more commonly a feminine accomplishment. The altar-cloth illustrated in plate 83 is known to have been worked by a sailor who was incapacitated by falling from the mast of his ship. This man received instruction from a lady who was herself gifted and skilled in needlework, but he must have had some basic ability, together with the will to learn. This altar-cloth has no maritime motifs on it, but the embroidery shown in plate 27, on the other hand, although its history is not known, is clearly the work of a sailor, judging by subject and sentiment. Also, it is worked on a

'silk', that is to say the black kerchief worn by a sailor, formerly bound about his head in action as described in Chapter 3.

There is one particular article of his own on which a sailor might use decorative needlework, and that is the sailmaker's 'tidy', which is a square of canvas, supported by its top edge, having rows of pouches in it, for the safe keeping of such things as seam rubbers, needles, and sailmaker's 'palms'. I remember seeing a good specimen of this article about 1936, aboard a cruiser I served in, and there is one in the National Maritime Museum at Greenwich.

Perhaps the most interesting of all sailors' work, and a subject about which little has been written, is wool pictures. These are usually of ships, although patriotic symbols

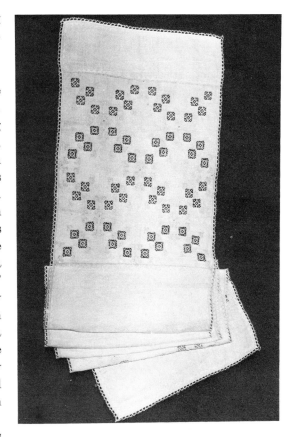

83 Altar cloth of linen, edged with crochet and with openwork at each end. Breadth 2ft. Early twentieth century

and other subjects are known. They are worked in crewel of long and short stitches. The backing is sailcloth, the stitching normally of wool but occasionally of silk, with the rigging done in cotton and linen threads. In rare examples, cuttlefish pens have been shaped and used to fill the sails. The stretcher commonly has simple tenon joints, without wedges, and the frame is usually of maple wood, with a gilt inlay. The names of the ships are often shown, as is a date, but seldom is the name of the 'artist' given. As to the dates, the great majority are in the third quarter of the nineteenth century, when there must have been quite a craze for wool pictures, and it is remarkable that there are no well-known literary references to them. Scrimshaw, of around the same time, is freely mentioned in whaling-ship logs and reminiscences.

It has been suggested that these pictures were made by professional artists to the order of seafaring men, but I find this hard to believe. The whole spirit of them is amateur folk art, and sailorly attention is paid to the rigging, which in good examples is made of several different thicknesses of thread, as dictated by the original ropes' use. A more likely possibility expressed to me is that they were an early example of 'occupational therapy' at the sailors' hospital at Greenwich. Certainly in World War I the wounded were provided with perforated cards, blunt needles and a supply of wool, so that they might sew patriotic motifs, the flags of the Allies and so on. These might have been the degenerate descendants of wool pictures. It is my own suggestion that inspiration for wool pictures came from the

Chinese embroideries sold to sailors in Hong Kong and the Treaty Ports, opened to the West in 1842. The height of the craze for wool pictures in the third quarter of the nineteenth century agrees with this theory, and I once owned an embroidery of the Royal Arms which had every appearance of being native Chinese work of about 1850. The fashion for wool pictures never 'caught on' in the USA, but they are avidly collected in America now, and rightly so as they are objects of considerable charm and interest.

A favourite subject is one or other of the last of the wooden battleships, and ironclads with auxiliary steam power are also often depicted. It seems that nostalgia for the days of sail may have played some part in their making. For instance plate 23 shows the

84 Wool picture of an un-named battleship with attendant steam tug, made probably in the late 1850s. Sight size 30in by 25in

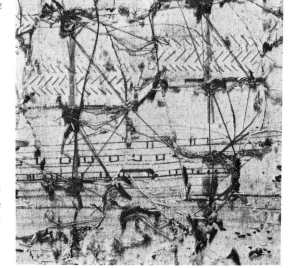

85 Part view of the back of the wool picture shown in plate 24. The artist made an ink sketch of the ship on this side of the canvas, but for some reason rejected it and finally used the other side instead

86 Wool picture of six ships, made about 1855. Sight size 38in by 21in

87 Wool picture of an un-named ship, dated on grounds of style to the 1860s. This appears to be a merchantman, in 'Nelson chequer'. Sight size 18in by 15in

88 *Wool picture titled* Our iron clad fleet— HMS Minutar, Hercules, Agincourt, Inconstant—*passing the Fairon and Holy Islands. All these ships were iron screw-driven ships which joined the British fleet late in the 1860s. This picture probably worked about 1870. Sight size 40in by 25in*

4th rate HMS *Arethusa*, which was out of the Navy List in 1872, but the picture is dated 1875. Again, the steam frigate HMS *Terrible* was re-engined soon after her completion in 1846 to give her four funnels, but the wool picture (plate 26) which is dated 1864 shows the less obtrusive two funnels of the ship as first put into service.

Plate 84 shows a ship dressed with flags 'over all' as the saying is. The string of flags hanging from the extreme ends of the ship are not fanciful, as might be thought. They show the practice of leading the dressing lines down to the water's edge by suspending sounding leads from the flying jib boom and

the driver boom, to complete the effect of a rainbow of colours outlining the vessel.

The technique of working these pictures was to set up the canvas and ink the outlines of the ship or ships, as shown in plate 85. It will be noticed that only the ship and its rigging are outlined; the sea, sky, and other incidentals were to be sewn in freehand, and indeed the finished article gives evidence of this in the charming liberties taken with the appearance of these elements.

Wool pictures can be made which at first glance will pass for originals, but they are not extensively faked as it is difficult to give a convincing look of age to the stretcher and canvas, and the colours of new wool will appear unnaturally bright. Of course the newly-sewn picture could be 'antiqued', but even so careful examination should detect the fake, particularly by comparison between the exposed areas and the parts protected by the frame.

The last four plates (86 to 89) have been

placed in a suggested order of date, derived so far as possible from what is known of the ships depicted, but with some regard for style. The later pictures are coarser, particularly in the size of threads for the rigging, and a typical late nineteenth-century use of 'space fillers' in the use of meaningless small ships and boats may be detected. The joker in the pack is plate 89. I can find no ketch named *Speculator* recorded around 1872, the

89 Wool picture of a ketch, titled Speculator 1872, *and possibly work of that period. Sight size 26in by 19in*

shadows on the sea look a little too sophisticated, and the paddle tug in the background is unconvincing. Nevertheless the picture has no obvious faults, and I have therefore included it as an interesting rarity among the more usual ships of war.

GLOSSARY

Burgee   a flag of normal proportions, but with a 'vee' cut in the side furthest from the mast

Caboose   some nook appropriated for his use by a sailor, probably a petty officer or a specialist such as a sailmaker

Chains   the ledges on the sides of sailing ships to which the ropes supporting the mast, known as shrouds, were attached

Course   the lowest sail on each of the masts of a square rigged ship

Deadrise   in effect, the depth of keel: a flat bottomed vessel has no deadrise

Driver, or Spanker   a large fore-and-aft sail set low on the after-mast in square rigged ships

Fid   a tapered wooden pin, used for separating the parts or strands of a rope in knotting and splicing

Flensing deck   the deck where the whales' blubber is cut off

Orlop deck   the deck over the hold, below the lower gun deck in a warship. The word is derived from 'overlap', as it overlaps the hold

Pan-bone   the dense bone of a sperm whale's jaw

Pendant   a flag of long, trailing shape. This is the correct spelling, but 'pennant' is the preferred pronunciation, by elision of the double consonant, and it has become the accepted spelling

Poop   a short raised deck aft, from which to control the ship

Royals   the topmost square sails, except in clipper ships

Sailmaker's palm   a pad of leather held in the palm of the hand to assist in driving the needle through canvas

Scrimshaw   the folk art of the whaling seaman, mostly engravings and carvings on bone, ivory and wood, during the great days of ocean whaling from 1820 to 1914

Sheer   the degree of slope up of the ship's side towards the bow and stern

Stanchion   a pillar, of iron or brass, supporting the guard rails round the weather deck of a ship

Steeved   said of a bowsprit with an angle above the horizontal

Studding sails   extra sails set outboard of the principal square sails when the wind permits. Pronounced 'stun'sls'. The word probably derives from the broad headed nails formerly used to stud the ship's side below the waterline

Truck   the round wooden piece on top of a mast

Try-pot   the boiler in which blubber is rendered down into oil

Woolding   rope or sennit wound round a composite mast to hold it together

BIBLIOGRAPHY

Ashley, C. W. *Book of Knots*. New York: Doubleday Doran, 1944

Barrière and Leland. *Dictionary of Slang*. London: George Bell, 1897

Baynham, Henry. *From the Lower Deck*. London: Hutchinson, 1969

——. *Before the Mast*. London: Hutchinson, 1971

Brown, D. G. *The Floating Bulwark*. London: Cassell, 1963

Carr, H. Gresham (ed). *Flags of the World*. London: Frederick Warne, 1956

Chatterton, Keble. *The Old East Indiaman*. London: Conway Maritime Press, 1971

Concise Encyclopaedia of Antiques. Compiled by *The Connoisseur*. London: Rainbird, 1960

Dillmont, Th de. *Encyclopaedia of Needlework*. DMC Library, 1907

Edlin, Herbert. *What Wood Is That?* London: Thames & Hudson, 1969

Flayderman, E. N. *Scrimshaw and Scrimshanders*. Flayderman, 1972

Frere-Cook, Gervis (ed). *The Decorative Arts of the Mariner*. London: Cassell, 1966

Lever's Seamanship. Thomas Gill, 1808

Hansen, H. J. *Art and the Seafarer*. London: Faber & Faber, 1968

Hensel, R. G. and J. *Encyclopaedia of Knots and Fancy Ropework*. New York: Cornell Maritime Press, 1952

Hodges, H. W. and Hughes, E. A. *Select Naval Documents*. London: Cambridge University Press, 1922

Jarrett, Dudley. *British Naval Dress*. London: Dent, 1960

Kemp, Peter. *The British Sailor*. London: Dent, 1970

Kipping. *Sails and Sailmaking*. London: Virtue, 1865

Lambert, M. and Marx, Enid. *English Popular Art*. London: Batsford, 1957

Landstrom, Bjorn. *The Ship*. London: Allen & Unwin, 1961

Lubbock, Basil. *The Western Ocean Packets*. Glasgow: Brown Son & Ferguson, 1925

——. *The China Clippers*. Glasgow: Brown Son & Ferguson, 1946

——. *The Blackwall Frigates*. Glasgow: Brown Son & Ferguson, 1948

——. *The Colonial Clippers*. Glasgow: Brown Son & Ferguson, 1948

Macintyre, Donald. *The Man of War*. London: Methuen, 1968

Manual of Seamanship (1926). HM Stationery Office

Masefield, John. *Sea Life in Nelson's Time*. London: Conway Maritime Press, 1971

Matthews, Dr D. H. (ed). *The Whale*. London: Allen & Unwin, 1968

Paul, Nicholas. *Diary of a Clerk in HMS Vanguard 1836 to 1839*. Unpublished MS

Perrin, W. G. *British Flags*. London: Cambridge University Press, 1922

Spencer, Charles L. *Knots, Splices and Fancy Work*. Glasgow: Brown Son & Ferguson, 1937

Steel, David. *The Elements and Practice of Rigging and Seamanship*. London, 1794

Thomas, Hugh. *Cuba*. London: Eyre & Spottiswoode, 1971

SOURCES OF ILLUSTRATIONS

For the skill and care of several professional photographers whose work appears in this book I am most grateful, and I would like to record a special word of thanks to two amateur photographers, Kenneth Grinstead and Michael Fatherly.

Most of the line illustrations are by Michael Ellis, who worked patiently in a field unfamiliar to him. Acknowledgement is due to Alec A. Purves for the illustration of Marryat's flags, to F. A. Herbig-Verlagebuchhandlung, Berlin for the illustration from *Costume through the Ages*, and to E. Norman Flayderman for permission to adapt the illustration on p 86 of his book *Scrimshaw and Scrimshanders*.

Acknowledgement is also due to the following for permission to reproduce photographs. The numbers refer to the plates.

By courtesy of: Birmingham City Museum & Art Gallery, 25, 46, 51, 52, 68; City of Salford Museum, 16, 74; City and County of Kingston Upon Hull Museums, 4, 19, 44, 54, 65, 76; Dartmouth Museum, 20; Dundee Corporation Museums, 39, 50, 55, 57, 63, 72, 73; HMS Victory Museum, 12; National Maritime Museum, Frontispiece, 15, 45; Portsmouth City Museums, 3; Southampton Museums, 21, 81; Tonbridge Museum, 17, 48

By courtesy of: The Parker Gallery, 2, 29, 30, 56; University of California, 33, 34

By courtesy of: Mrs Raymond Bonham-Carter, 22, 24, 26, 28, 84, 85, 86, 87, 88, 89; W. H. C. Blake, 5, 10, 31; J. Stevens Cox, 35; Clive Lloyd, 6, 60, 64, 66, 69; Sir Aymer Maxwell, Bt., 13; Robert Newall, 83; Mrs E. Q. Nicholson, 32; Mrs Jo Petersen, 1, 18, 43; Commander J. E. Smallwood, OBE, RN, 62

Author's Collection: 7, 23, 27, 36, 40, 41, 42, 47, 49, 58, 59, 61, 67, 70, 71, 77, 78, 79, 80

ACKNOWLEDGEMENTS

I have had advice and help from many people, and would express my gratitude to the following in particular: members of the Staff of the National Maritime Museum and Admiralty Library; Mr F. Richardson of the Royal Botanical Gardens at Kew; Mr R. E. Taylor of the Brixham Museum; Mr Bertram Newbury of the Parker Gallery, London; Mr P. F. Purrington of the Whaling Museum, New Bedford, Massachusetts; Mr T. Richardson of the Dartmouth Museum, Devon; Mr J. Stevens Cox of St Peter Port, Guernsey; Mr Douglas V. Duff, Mrs Charlotte Johnson, Mr N. Dalton-Clifford and Miss Marguerite Steen.

I have been given sage advice; I have read books and manuscripts; I have travelled to meet people and see things; I have considered what conclusions can be justifiably derived. If despite all that I have made mistakes then I can only plead as Dr Johnson did, when the lady asked why he had defined the pastern as the knee of a horse, 'Ignorance, madam, pure ignorance'.

Finally my most grateful thanks are due to Mrs Joan Hickmott, who transformed my untidy MS into an elegant typescript.

INDEX